Nonnie
Talks about
Sex...& More

Suggested for children in grades
5-8 and their trusted adults

An Interactive Book for Children and Adults	By Dr. Mary Jo Podgurski

Illustrations by Alice M. Burroughs

NONNIE TALKS ABOUT SEX..& MORE: VOLUME SIX OF THE NONNIE SERIES

The Academy for Adolescent Health,Inc. website is http://healthyteens.com/

Illustrations created by Alice Burroughs are the property of the Academy for Adolescent Health, Inc. and are copyright protected. All rights reserved.

Photographs were purchased for use in this book or were donated and used with permission, for exclusive use in this book.

ISBN-13: 978-1979306485
ISBN-10: 1979306486

Dedications

I taught my first sexuality education in 1981.
From 1988—2013, my team and I taught
over 230,000 young people in-school,
quality, interactive, reality-based sexuality education.
Since 1995, we have trained over 15,000 teens as peer
educators. This is for them.

With special gratitude to
Dr. Dennis Dailey
for permission to use
the Circles of Sexuality. Thank you!

Shout out to Dr. Sol Gordan, who taught us all about love in his book,
How Can You Tell If You're Really in Love

I am deeply grateful to my wise friend, Bill Taverner, MA,
for his role as consultant author

With gratitude to our reviewers:
Elizabeth Crane, Ph.D.
Dennis Dailey, DSW
Joan Garrity, Consultant and Trainer
Shadeen Francis, MFT
Mariotta Gary-Smith, MPH
Anastasia Higginbotham, Author
Michael McGee, Ph.D.
Bill Selverstone, Ph.D.
Al Vernacchio, MA

Special kudos to our youth focus group and peer educator reviewers,
and to Robby and Christopher Taverner.
Young people's perspectives rock!

Introduction: Thoughts about a Child's Developmental Readiness for the Nonnie Series:

Many people ask me for help in determining a child's readiness for the books in the *Nonnie Series*.

Children today can glean information from online sources in a mouse click or smartphone search, but they are not always as comfortable sharing their concerns with adults. Adults, conversely, may not know how to address complicated topics, or may think a child is "too young" or unaware. I think the power of the *Nonnie Series* is the message "It's OK to talk about this together" – for adults and children!

Monitor your children's ability to process information. Maturity and age are often unrelated to reading ability; an adult can read and explain complicated words and concepts, but a child's curiosity and eagerness to embrace knowledge are important considerations. Adults need to "articulate the obvious" when educating children. It's important to empower. Try paraphrasing this message: "I'd like to look at this book with you. I think you may be interested in the topic. We can read the book at your own pace. You can talk with me about anything, and I will respect you."

I suggest grade levels as opposed to age because I'm sensitive to reading ability, but I truly do not feel the books should be limited to one group. I suggest 5th—8th graders for this book, but a few 3rd or 4th graders may be developmentally ready; the books should be read at a child's speed. Please know that I based my suggestions on the reality of children's lives in technology in today's world.

No one is more important to a child than a trusted adult. Learning takes place when we process information; communicate with the young people in your lives and share your values with respect.

Each child is different. Let your children lead you. Their interest, more than their grade level or age, should be your guide.

Thank you for listening and caring about young people.

With respect and admiration,

Mary Jo Podgurski

Nonnie
Talks about
Sex...& More

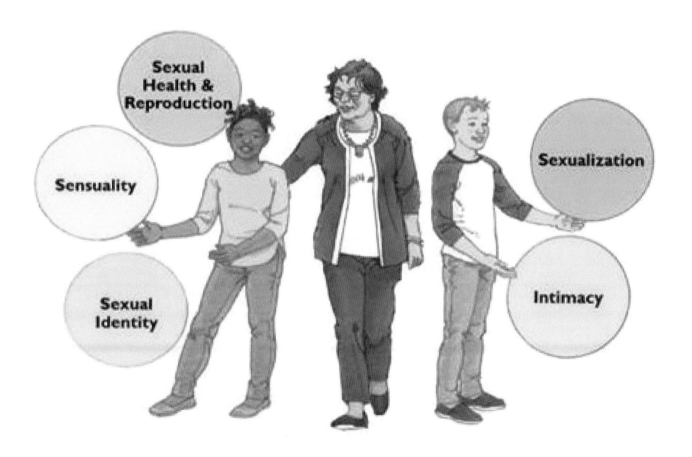

Sexual Health & Reproduction

Sensuality

Sexual Identity

Sexualization

Intimacy

Suggested for children in grades 5-8 and their trusted adults

An Interactive Book for Children and Adults

By Dr. Mary Jo Podgurski
Illustrations by Alice M. Burroughs

HOW TO USE THIS BOOK:

Nonnie Talks about Sex & More was created to be used by young people and adults together. Please read this book with someone who matters to you.

For Young People:
This picture means you may color the page if you wish. People of all ages enjoy coloring. This symbol * or a red word means a word may be new. The Glossary on pages 130-137 will help with new words that are especially important messages for you, the reader.

A What Do YOU think? page is a great page to help people talk with each other.
Please talk with a trusted adult!
Please listen!

Most important:
Every person is different. Each child who picks up this book is different. Each adult who reads this book with a child is different.
Some ideas may be easy to understand. That's OK.
Some ideas may be difficult to understand. That's OK.

     AcademyPress ~ www.healthyteens.com

HOW TO USE THIS BOOK:

FOR PARENTS, TEACHERS AND OTHER TRUSTED ADULTS:

1. I strongly recommend reading the book without your child first. Consider any concerns you may have with the material and prepare for your child's possible questions.
2. The book is divided into chapters. The chapters are only suggestions; they divide the content to allow for pleasant learning. The book may be read as one part, two parts, three parts, four parts—it's up to you. You know your children best. Please monitor their attention, their interest, and their awareness and understanding of the concepts.
3. The topic of sex may be controversial. Trusted adults in a child's family are uniquely positioned to convey this information, along with values and rationale for those values. I recommend this book for grades 5—8, but I believe pieces of the book would be useful for younger, inquisitive children.
4. Technology places us in a complicated place as educators. Most of my students in grades 5 and 6 use cell phones with online access. My younger students often have tablets. The scenario of Annie was created from a real life situation. I didn't change anything except the child's name.
5. Just as children's physical and emotional development are unique, so is their readiness for information. Please let the children you love be your guides.
6. The language in the book purposefully is inclusive of all genders.
7. The What Do YOU Think? pages should be completed at a young person's pace, but are important. Learning takes place when we process information.

Most important:

Be aware of the "music" (tone of voice) behind your words. If your child decides to read the book alone, please follow up and discuss the contents. Adult modeling and acceptance of skills like respect and empathy are vital.

Please teach children the importance of respect.
Each Person is a Person of Worth.
Please pass it on!

Mary Jo Podgurski

   AcademyPress ~ www.healthyteens.com

Chapter One: The Story Begins

Did you ever have a
huge question?

Most children wonder about a lot of different things.

Would you like to read a story
about two children with lots of questions?
The story may answer some of your
questions.

If you still have questions when the story is finished,
please ask your parents or a
trusted adult.

1

   AcademyPress ~ www.healthyteens.com

Once upon a time….

Alex and Tamika are best friends.

They can't remember a time when they weren't friends.

Their parents said they were even in the same play group when they were only two years old!

AcademyPress ~ www.healthyteens.com

Tamika and Alex are growing older. They are now in 6th grade. They love their families.

Tamika lives with her Mom and Dad. Her older brother LeBron is in college, so sometimes she goes to his empty room to be alone (unless he's home on break). Being alone makes Tamika feel calm*. Sometimes, 6th grade is challenging*.

Alex lives with his Dad, his Stepmom, and his little sister Alisia. He spends a lot of time with his dog, Mac. He sleeps at his Mom's house every other week-end. Alex likes to be outside, especially when it's noisy in his house. His sister often plays loudly!

Being alone makes Alex feel calm. He thinks 6th grade is challenging at times, too.

Do you like to be alone?
What is challenging in your life?

3

What Do YOU Think?

Growing up can be confusing.

What is confusing about growing up?
How do you act when you're confused?

Please draw
or write your
thoughts
here:

AcademyPress ~ www.healthyteens.com

Since they were small, Tamika and Alex have been curious* children.

They are also lucky. It's like they won a big jackpot*! Nonnie tells them they won the "parenting lottery*!"

They have parents and families who support them and love them. They know their families are a gift, and they are happy they have so many trusted adults in their lives.

A trusted adult* is someone who respects young people, listens to their thoughts and words, and keeps promises.

Alex's grandma is called Nonnie.

She's a nurse and a teacher and a counselor. When the children are confused about something or are curious about life, they often talk with Nonnie. She listens to them, respects them, and helps them grow and learn. She is a trusted adult.

5

AcademyPress ~ www.healthyteens.com

Except…

Lately, Tamika and Alex are moody*.

They know why they're moody. Nonnie taught them about puberty*.
They know:
1. Their hormones* are changing.
2. Their emotions* (feelings) are changing.
3. Their bodies are changing*.

They're also moody because their friends are going through puberty and they're moody! One of the strongest moods is anger.

So…even though they still love their families, they don't always LIKE them.
Sometimes, their families annoy them.

Like, when Tamika's Mom asks, *"Who are your friends now, Tamika?'*
Or, when Alex's Dad asks, *"What happened in school today, son?"*

If someone says, *"Have a nice day,"* they often want to scream!

*See *Nonnie Talks about Puberty* for more info.

AcademyPress ~ www.healthyteens.com

One day, they came home from school acting very angry.

Tamika stormed into her house, slamming the door behind her. Her parents were confused by her behavior*.

Alex was also angry. He slammed the door as he entered his house, too. His parents were just as confused as Tamika's parents!

AcademyPress ~ www.healthyteens.com

What do you think happened?

Have you ever felt angry?

If you've felt angry, what made you feel mad?

How long did the anger last?

 What did you do to move past the anger?

There are times when parents and trusted adults are confused, just like Tamika's and Alex's parents. They don't know why a young person is angry.

What do you wish parents and trusted adults would do or say when they see you are angry?

Sometimes young people don't share their feelings, especially if they're hiding something. Some people, of all ages, lock away their anger or their sadness deep inside, almost as if they hide it inside secret boxes.

Do you think Tamika and Alex could be hiding something? Why do you think they are angry?

AcademyPress ~ www.healthyteens.com

Tamika's Mom tried to talk with her. Tamika didn't want to share the reason for her anger. Tamika was angry because she was troubled. She was angry because she was trying to make a difficult decision.

Alex's Dad tried to talk with him. Alex didn't want to share the reason for his anger either. Alex was angry because he was troubled. He was angry because he didn't know how to support Tamika's decision.

AcademyPress ~ www.healthyteens.com

What Do YOU Think?

What do you think happened in Tamika's and Alex's life?
Do you think they have a secret?

Do you think they're in trouble?
Why do you think they might not share with their parents?

Please draw
or write your
thoughts
here:

AcademyPress ~ www.healthyteens.com

Chapter Two: In Trouble!

In time, it seems as if most secrets are discovered, no matter how deep they are hidden.

Tamika and Alex didn't understand. They didn't share their secret, because they were afraid. They thought their parents would be angry. They might be, but keeping secrets doesn't make a parent less angry. The children hid their fear with their own anger.

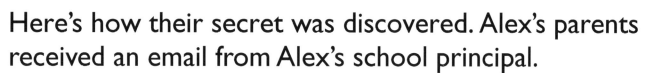

Alex and Tamika needed to tell the truth.

Here's how their secret was discovered. Alex's parents received an email from Alex's school principal.

Alex didn't know the email arrived, but he soon was told.

Alex was in trouble!

Something happened at school and he didn't share the situation with his parents.

 AcademyPress ~ www.healthyteens.com

At almost the same time, Tamika's parents received an identical* email from her school principal.

Tamika didn't know the email arrived, but her parents quickly told her.

Tamika was in trouble, too!

She kept a secret from her parents, just like Alex.

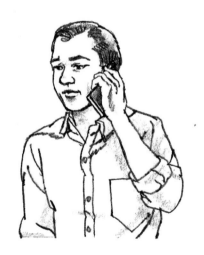

Since the parents are good friends, they called each other right away.

They decided they would deal with the situation together.

AcademyPress ~ www.healthyteens.com

The next day, Tamika and Alex and their parents met with their school principal, Ms. Keen.

The secret was out!

Nude pics* were found on Tamika's and Alex's phones.

When the principal asked them why the pictures were on their phones, they answered quickly.

"I didn't ask for the pic," Tamika protested.

"Me either," said Alex. "It just came to my phone."

The principal was very serious.
"Who sent the pictures to you?" she asked both young people.

Alex looked at Tamika.

Tamika looked at Alex.

"I don't know," said Alex.

"I don't know either," said Tamika.

The principal shook her head. "Everyone involved in this mess is saying the same thing," she said.
"No one will admit who started sending nude pictures."

Tamika's Dad said, "Both of you know right from wrong. We expected you to tell one of us you received these pictures." Tamika's Mom added, "I thought you knew better."

Alex's Mom agreed, "Why did you keep them on your phones?" she asked. "We spoke about this. You knew it's illegal*." Alex's Dad said, "I'm disappointed in you both."

All the adults were staring at Tamika and Alex.

AcademyPress ~ www.healthyteens.com

 Alex looked miserable*.
So did Tamika.
It seemed as if everyone they loved was upset with them.

Ms. Keen said, "We've discovered the picture isn't a pic of one of our students. One of our students photoshopped* her own face on a pic of a nude woman's body she found online."

Tamika brightened a little, "So, no one was really hurt?"

Ms. Keen said, "Someone was definitely hurt. You know who was hurt."

Alex squirmed in his seat, and Tamika looked away.

Finally, Tamika said, "We didn't believe the pic was Annie's. We heard she sent a nude pic with her face on it, but..."

 "Did you defend your friend?" Ms. Keen asked. "Did you tell Annie people were sharing her picture without permission?"

Alex mumbled, "No."

AcademyPress ~ www.healthyteens.com

Ms. Keen added, "The picture was shared throughout our school and in the high school."

Tamika whispered, "You're right Mom, we knew better." Alex agreed.

How can you be a good person?

Their parents were even more confused. They thought Tamika and Alex knew how to be good people. They were taught to support their friends. They knew how important it was to talk with their parents.

The families left school together and stood outside by their cars. The parents had so many unanswered questions. They wondered, how did this happen?

Alex's Dad, Stepmom, and Mom met to discuss what would happen next. Tamika's Mom and Dad asked her if it was OK to call her brother LeBron to ask his opinion. She agreed. They all spoke together.

Everyone agreed there needed to be consequences* to the young people's actions.

problem responsibility deadline question decisions consequences

AcademyPress ~ www.healthyteens.com

Chapter Three: Consequences

Consequences happen when someone makes a mistake*. Here is what happened:

1. Both Annie (who sent the pic), and the boy who requested she send the pic, and then shared it, were suspended* from school for 3 days.
2. Everyone at school who was involved in sending or receiving the nude pic received detention*.
3. Both Alex and Tamika were grounded* by their parents for a week.
4. Annie, Alex and Tamika all lost the use of their phones indefinitely*.

It was very quiet at their houses the rest of the week. Alex and Tamika were sad and angry, even though their parents tried to make them feel loved. They felt many things—anger, because they didn't understand why they got into so much trouble, and guilt*, because they didn't help Annie.

Tamika told her Mom it was as if their houses were covered in snow and ice.

Alex told his Dad he felt alone and cold, even though the weather was warm. Since they live in California, the children seldom see snow. Alex told Tamika he felt like his bedroom window was covered in ice. Tamika agreed.

What Do YOU Think?

Were the consequences Alex and Tamika faced fair*?

Let's play a game. It's called Role Play.
Pretend to be the parent of an 11-year-old who sent a nude pic to someone. What would you do?

Please draw or write your thoughts here:

AcademyPress ~ www.healthyteens.com

Tamika and Alex talked during lunch at school.

They remembered who answered their questions when they started puberty. Alex's Nonnie taught them about their bodies and growing up.

They thought about their confusion when they were younger and they encountered* racism. Nonnie and her two friends, Marti and Renee, helped them sort out complicated* feelings.

They remembered when their aunts had their baby cousins. Nonnie helped them understand pregnancy and birth.

They thought about Nonnie's support when Alex's dog died and Tamika's abuelito* was very sick. She taught them about death.

19

Finally, both young people made a decision.

They asked their parents if they could spend some time talking with Nonnie.

Their parents agreed. Nonnie was teaching other teachers in Chicago.

Tamika's parents, Alex's parents, and her brother LeBron connected with Nonnie online and talked for a while. Alex's Dad, who was Nonnie's son, said, "We'd like you to talk with them."

Nonnie was happy to spend time with Tamika and Alex when she returned home.

 AcademyPress ~ www.healthyteens.com

As soon as she arrived, Nonnie did something Tamika and Alex did not expect.

She asked them for their friend Annie's phone number.

First, Nonnie spoke with Annie's Mom. Alex was surprised by how much Nonnie was silent, just listening. Then, Nonnie spoke with Annie. Tamika and Alex watched.

When she hung up, Nonnie told Tamika and Alex, "I'm glad you reached out to me." She smiled and added, "Thanks for waiting while I spoke with Annie and her Mom. I'm not upset with you. You're both good people."

Tamika was shocked. "Aren't you mad at us, Nonnie?" she asked, afraid of the answer.

"Of course not," Nonnie said.
Alex frowned, "Why not? Everyone else is mad at us."

Nonnie shook her head, still smiling. "No, Alex. People are just worried. They want you both to do the right thing. I know you two. It will be OK."

 AcademyPress ~ www.healthyteens.com

Alex said, "How can you say it will be OK?" He sounded angry. When Tamika added, "Everyone hates us," she sounded angry, too. "Nothing will be OK again," she said.

"You made a mistake," Nonnie said. "I don't know a single person who manages to live without making mistakes." She hugged both young people. "What matters is how we learn from our mistakes. You can grow from this mistake."

Tamika rolled her eyes. "We've heard that before. From our parents…"
"And from Ms. Keen," Alex interrupted. "Nonnie, we thought you would be different."

Nonnie's voice was warm and her touch on their shoulders was gentle. "I know," she said calmly. "We'll figure this out together." She wasn't upset when they sounded angry. She waited a moment, spending time with them. They were quiet together for a little while. Tamika remembered Nonnie comforting them when they were small.
She looked at Alex and said, "Maybe Nonnie is different. No one else said we'll be OK."

Alex sounded young when he said, "Will we be OK?"

AcademyPress ~ www.healthyteens.com

Chapter Four: Annie

Nonnie said, "Absolutely. I have faith in you both." She was quiet again, and then she asked, "Isn't there a person who is hurt by this more than you two?"

The young people immediately thought of Annie. They felt guilty once more. Tamika asked, "Why did you call Annie? Why did you talk with her Mom?"

Nonnie said, "I wanted to reach out to Annie. I know she's troubled. Her parents are, too. I'd like to share some of our time together with Annie. Would you be OK if we invited her to join us?" Tamika and Alex talked together. They'd been trying to talk with Annie since this happened, but they didn't know what to say. "Yes," they both said.

 AcademyPress ~ www.healthyteens.com

They walked up and down the beach, until Nonnie got tired and needed to rest. While she sat on the beach, Tamika, Alex and Annie played in the surf.

Then they walked some more.

They talked about many things.

They talked about their favorite movies. Tamika likes scary movies more than Alex. He likes movies where things explode. Annie listened.

They talked about their favorite school subjects. Alex likes English, because he wants to be a writer some day.

Tamika likes science.
She thinks she wants to be a veterinarian like her Aunt Janell.

Annie just listened.

They shared their favorite foods...spaghetti, hamburgers, salad, fries, pizza, and chicken tenders. Tamika and Alex agreed about foods! Annie still listened.

    AcademyPress ~ www.healthyteens.com

Talking about food made them hungry.

Nonnie took them to a small food shack on the boardwalk. They ordered fries with ketchup, burgers, pizza, and lemonade.

For dessert, they enjoyed funnel cakes.

As they ate, Annie seemed a little less tense. Nonnie was pleased. She was waiting for Annie to feel OK.

Tamika looked at Alex and Alex looked at Tamika.

They were impatient*. It felt like waiting in line for tickets to a concert. It felt like standing in the cafeteria line waiting for lunch.

Tamika said, "Nonnie, we've been talking for hours! We've talked about everything but the nude pics."

Alex asked Nonnie, "What's wrong with you?" He'd never seen her take so long to talk about something!

 AcademyPress ~ www.healthyteens.com

Nonnie smiled, and asked Alex to buy her a hot tea. Of course, he did. She sipped it slowly, while Tamika and Alex glared* at her and Annie looked uneasy. Finally, she sighed. "What a lovely afternoon," she said.

"What!?" said Tamika.

"Nonnie," Alex said, "why aren't you scolding us?"

Annie suddenly looked afraid, until Nonnie said, "Why do you think I should scold you?"

All three children stared at her, and Nonnie shook her head. "I think," she said, "you are very bright children. I think you know what you need."

"We need your help," Tamika whined, and Nonnie nodded. "Perhaps," she said. "I want you to think about how to make sense of what happened. Life is full of lessons. Right now, I think you're angry and confused because you don't know what you did wrong. I'd like to meet once a week. The next time I see you, I want each of you to bring me one word you can use to help learn about respecting others online."

"What are the words, Nonnie?" Alex asked, frowning.

26 AcademyPress ~ www.healthyteens.com

Nonnie said, "If I tell you, Alex, you won't learn. Think back on our many talks. I will help you process* and understand the words you bring to me, but you will decide what you need."

Nonnie led the children to her car and drove them home. On the way, she sang to songs on the radio. Badly. Nonnie has many gifts, but singing in tune is not one of them.

The three children talked about their words every day at school.

They met exactly one week after their walk on the beach. Nonnie has an office in her house. Their parents dropped them off there.

Nonnie prepared an after-school snack of fruit and cheese and veggies.

Soft music played in the background as they ate.

A whiteboard and markers were ready for them.

AcademyPress ~ www.healthyteens.com

What Do YOU Think?

The children thought Nonnie was acting strangely.

Why do you think Nonnie waited to talk about the pics?
Why wouldn't she just give the children the words?
What words do you think would teach a lesson
about showing respect online?

Please draw
or write your
thoughts
here:

28

AcademyPress ~ www.healthyteens.com

Chapter Five: Guidelines

Nonnie said, "Let's set some guidelines for our time together." She turned to Annie and added, "Guidelines are the promises I make when I teach. Today, you will teach each other."

Alex added, "And you'll teach us."

Nonnie smiled. "You're growing up, Alex. Yes, I will teach you, but the real wisdom* for learning will come from each of you."
The three children thought about her words. Tamika said, "We should start with guidelines then. The first is respect, right?"

Nonnie was pleased. "Correct. Any others?" Alex said, "We won't judge one another." He suddenly realized how much this guideline meant to him. "Thank you for the 'not judging' us, Nonnie."

"Of course," Nonnie smiled. "Anything else?"

"We should have fun," Alex added, and Tamika agreed.

"We need to keep confidentiality*," Tamika said.

"Which means?" Nonnie asked. She turned to the children's friend and asked, "Annie, what do you think?"

Annie gave a tiny smile. "I think it means we don't share what anyone says."

Tamika gave her a hug. "Yep. Except if someone shares something huge, and Nonnie needs to get help. She'll tell us how she's going to share then. Right, Nonnie?"

Nonnie beamed, she was so happy. "Right, Tamika. Any more guidelines?"

 Alex grinned. "We should laugh, because life is funny at times. We don't laugh at each other though."

Nonnie said, "Perfect! Who would like to share their word first?"

Alex chose a blue marker and wrote the word empathy* on the board. "I think this word, Nonnie," he said. "I thought of it because we learned about empathy when you taught us about gender*. We were younger*."

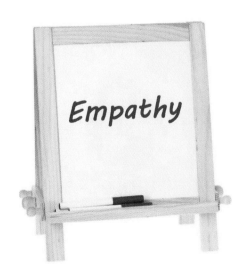

*See *Nonnie Talks about Gender* for more info.

AcademyPress ~ www.healthyteens.com

"Good choice, Alex," Nonnie said. "Why did you select empathy as your word?"

Alex squirmed a little, then he sighed. "I remember learning empathy from you before. I think we needed to have empathy." He glanced at Annie. "Empathy is about connection* and understanding." Alex looked at Tamika.

Tamika added, looking down. "If we had empathy for Annie, we would have gone to her right away. We would have told her…" she stopped, miserable. "Not supporting my friend was the biggest mistake I made."

Nonnie waited.

Annie finally asked, "Told me what?"

Alex mumbled, "Told you Ethan shared the pic you sent him."

Annie gasped. "Alex!" She looked shocked. "I never told anyone Ethan asked me for the pic! He did, but I never told."

Everyone was quiet.

AcademyPress ~ www.healthyteens.com

Nonnie reminded them gently, "Remember confidentiality, Annie. I won't share. You do know the school knows it was Ethan, right? He was suspended, too."

Annie blushed and said, "I know. It's so embarrassing*. I don't know why I sent it!"

Tamika asked, "How did he ask you?"

Annie squirmed and looked uncomfortable, until Alex said, "I know other people who ask for pics. Not just guys."

Annie felt better. She said in a voice so soft, Nonnie leaned forward to hear her better. "He texted me. He sent the words 'lemme c sum'."

Nonnie was confused, "How did you know what he wanted to see, Annie?" All three children grinned. "You're old, Nonnie," Alex said. He was confident Nonnie wouldn't be angry with him, since he was her grandson. "Everyone knows he wanted to see boobs."

"Oh," said Nonnie. "I knew this was about sex."

Annie gasped, "It's not about sex! I've never even kissed anyone."

AcademyPress ~ www.healthyteens.com

"Sexuality is about a lot more than sexual acts, Annie," said Nonnie. "I think you're ready to talk about sex. First let's look at the rest of your words. Empathy," she smiled at Alex, "is a great start."

"My word is honesty*," Tamika said, looking sheepish.

"A good word," Nonnie said. "Why did you select it?"

Tamika took a big breath. "I wasn't honest. I wish I said something. I could have told my Mom or my teacher. Or you, Nonnie. Instead, I did nothing."

"I did nothing as well, Tamika," Alex said, equally unhappy.

"Can you share why? Why didn't you tell? I promise not to judge you, no matter what you say," Nonnie said. "Telling the truth can be tough."

"I was afraid I'd be made fun of for telling," Tamika said. Alex agreed. "I didn't want to look like a loser who runs to his parents."

Annie blurted out, "I'm not being honest. Not now."

Everyone looked at her, curious. Annie looked miserable. She was quiet, but she looked as if she wanted to say something. She also looked as if she wanted to cry.

Tamika said, "You don't need to share if you don't feel ready, Annie." Nonnie smiled at Tamika and told Annie, "Tamika's correct, Annie."

Annie nodded. "I want to. I do." Then, she was quiet again. Nonnie said, "I think we need tea and cocoa." They went to Nonnie's kitchen. The children talked about a book they were reading for school while Nonnie made them drinks. Annie took a big breath, and said, "I like Ethan. I wanted him to like me. That's why I sent the pic to him." She wiped a few tears from her eyes.

AcademyPress ~ www.healthyteens.com

Everyone supported Annie. She shook her head back and forth, as if wishing she'd said no to Ethan's request*. "I looked in the bathroom mirror and saw I really didn't have any breasts."

"So you photoshopped your head on a nude picture with big breasts," Alex said. Annie just nodded.

Tamika snorted. "I don't have any breasts, either. Mom says I'm not grown yet."

Nonnie said, "Annie, thank you for sharing with us. Tamika, your Mom is right." She smiled at the children. "How brave you all are! This is why sending nude pics is linked to sexuality. Attraction* is normal. What is complicated* is how far each of us is willing to go to feel accepted by someone for whom we feel attraction."

Alex suddenly looked uncomfortable. "I'm attracted to someone, too, Nonnie."
Tamika grinned. "It's Logan, right?"
Alex glared. He looked like he wanted to hide.

Nonnie said, "Later, we'll talk about attraction and love and lust*." She looked at each child with kindness. "Remember, all of you. It's OK to think someone is attractive."

35

   AcademyPress ~ www.healthyteens.com

"Love!" said Tamika.

"Lust!" Alex shouted.

Nonnie grinned. "Not yet. I want to hear Annie's word."

Annie walked bravely to the white-board. She held the marker tightly. She took a great big breath, and wrote the word, regret*.

Nonnie said, "Choosing regret as your word took courage, Annie. Would you like to share why you selected it?"

Annie nodded, but was quiet. Tamika asked, "May I help?" And Annie said, yes very softly.

Tamika said, "I think regret means to feel badly about something a person does. I regret not telling you about Ethan." Alex agreed. "I regret not telling my Dad."

Annie looked relieved. "Do you really feel sad because you didn't speak up?" she asked.

Both children nodded solemnly. Tamika said, "We respect you. You're our friend." Tamika and Annie hugged.

AcademyPress ~ www.healthyteens.com

"We disappointed our parents by not telling them," Alex said. "So did I," said Annie sadly. Tamika said, "Worse than that, Annie. I disappointed you."

Nonnie said, "The first step to moving forward after a mistake is forgiving yourself. Forgiveness* from others, and forgiving yourself, may take time, but are important steps. What do you think should be your next step?"

"I'm honestly not sure," Annie said.

"For me, it's about letting a friend down and never doing it again," Tamika added, smiling at Annie, "I'm sorry."

Annie looked surprised, and gave Tamika a little smile.

Nonnie said, "Annie, it's OK if you're not sure what to do next right now. We'll all help each other figure things out. OK?"

"Annie and me and Tamika?" asked Alex. "We're not teachers." Nonnie said. "I have a training at our Teen Center this weekend. Who do you think I'm training?"

Alex grinned. "I think I know!" he said. "Peer educators*!"
Annie said, "What's a peer educator?"

"A young person who teaches with you, Nonnie," Tamika said. "Right?"

"Right," Nonnie said. "One of the best ways a young person can learn something is to teach it to peers. I want the three of you to help each other learn."

Excited, Tamika asked, "Are we old enough?"

"You're old enough to teach young people your age or younger, yes. Our teaching theme this year is about respecting others online. You would be great peer educators." She paused, thinking. "Next week, I'd like you to each bring in a new word." She began cleaning up the markers and erasing the white board.

 Alex and Tamika stopped her. "Wait a minute," Tamika said, "what about lust and love?"

"Yeah, Nonnie. And, sex. You mentioned sex," said Alex.

Nonnie laughed out loud. "I did. Let's talk about sex…"

Tamika interrupted, grinning, "baby…" she sang.

38 AcademyPress ~ www.healthyteens.com

Even Annie laughed, "What an old song, Tamika!" she said.

Nonnie continued, "Let's make sure Annie's parents are OK with this topic. Then, I'd like to teach you about the Circles of Sexuality*."

"Circles?" asked Tamika.

"Sexuality?" asked Alex.

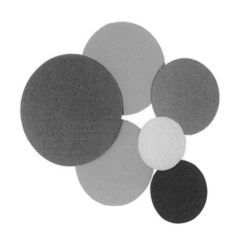 "Yes, Tamika," Nonnie smiled again. "Circles. My friends created a way of looking at sexuality involving five circles. Sexuality is more than just having sex, Alex. We can talk about it next week." She walked the children to the door. "Don't forget to bring your new words."

Curious, they began to walk home. Nonnie called out, "One more thing. Please explain the word holistic* when you return."

The children looked at each other. What a strange word!

They decided Nonnie was being difficult. They couldn't understand what this had to do with sending nude pics.

What Do YOU Think?

Holistic is a big word!

What do you think it means?
Why do you think Nonnie talks about sexuality
instead of just talking about sex?

Please draw
or write your
thoughts
here:

➡️

AcademyPress ~ www.healthyteens.com

Time passes differently for each person. The week moved quickly for Tamika. She was very busy with soccer and school.

The same amount of time seemed to go slowly for Alex. He missed having his phone. His parents weren't ready to return it.

The same seven days crawled for Annie. She wasn't hanging out with anyone except Alex and Tamika, and she only saw them at school and at Nonnie's. She didn't share any classes with them. She was lonely.

Nonnie visited Annie's home to talk with her mom and dad. Some adults are anxious* when their children learn about sex. Nonnie wanted to be sure Annie's parents were OK with their conversation.

Annie's parents were pleased. They gave Nonnie permission to talk about sex with Annie. Her dad said, "Sure. As long as I don't need to talk about that sex stuff!"

Mid-week, Nonnie called the children's families and changed the place where they would meet. She invited them to attend the class she taught at the local college.

41

They were welcomed into her college class. Nonnie taught her students about holistic sexuality.*

She explained how sexuality is part of life. She used cards to discuss the five Circles of Sexuality.

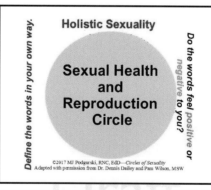

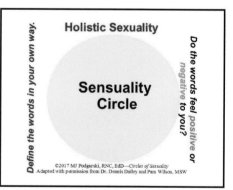

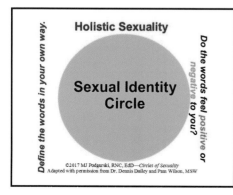

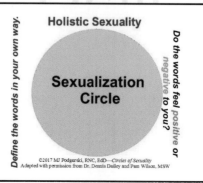

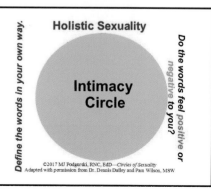

AcademyPress ~ www.healthyteens.com

When the class ended, she took the children to the campus coffee shop and ordered them milkshakes.

She ordered a fancy coffee. She asked, "Before we talk about my class, I'm curious. What words did you choose this week?"

Before anyone could answer, Tamika said, "Why do we keep talking about words, Nonnie?"

Nonnie smiled and asked, "Great question. Why do we?"

Tamika laughed, "I think you're trying to help us think!" Alex agreed. "I like words, though," he said.

"Words matter," Nonnie said. "I do want you to think."

Annie was quiet. Nonnie said, "I'm happy you're here, Annie."

Annie mumbled, "Me, too."

Alex said, "Let's play Roses and Thorns."

AcademyPress ~ www.healthyteens.com

Tamika and Alex explained how the game Roses and Thorns worked. Each person shares something OK about their week and something not OK. A person may also "pass" and be silent.

Annie surprised them all by speaking first, "I hated this week. I couldn't wait to be with you. People treat me like I'm a freak* at school."

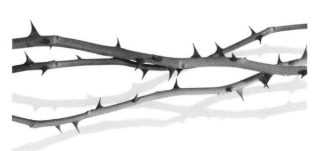

Nonnie nodded. "You shouldn't be treated poorly. Any roses, Annie? Any good things?"

Annie thought a moment, then shook her head. "Only looking forward to us getting together."

"That's something, Annie," Tamika smiled at her friend. "I'll go next. My rose is easy. We're going to talk about sex." She giggled nervously. "I don't have a thorn."

Alex grunted. "You always look for good things, Tamika. You're annoying*." He paused, thinking. "My rose is the same as yours, though." He gave Nonnie a crooked grin. "My thorn is missing my phone. My mom thinks phones are evil. I think I'll be 30 when I get mine back!"

44 AcademyPress ~ www.healthyteens.com

Chapter Seven: Talking about Sex

"How about you, Nonnie?" Alex asked. "Do you have a rose or a thorn?"

Nonnie said, "I'll pass. Today is about you. Shall we discuss your words first, or talk about sex first?"

"Sex!" said Tamika. "Sex!" said Alex.

Annie said in a small voice, "Sex...yes, sex first."

Nonnie said, "Agreed. Let's make a deal. Each time we meet we'll look at one of the Circles of Sexuality and then think about your words. You'll think about new words for each week, OK?"

The children said yes.

Nonnie gave each child a paper labeled Contract*.

Alex read the paper aloud. Alex looked up. "This is easy. I'll sign."

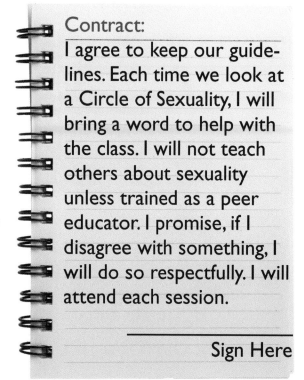

Contract:
I agree to keep our guidelines. Each time we look at a Circle of Sexuality, I will bring a word to help with the class. I will not teach others about sexuality unless trained as a peer educator. I promise, if I disagree with something, I will do so respectfully. I will attend each session.

_____
Sign Here

 AcademyPress ~ www.healthyteens.com

Alex, Tamika and Annie signed quickly, and Nonnie signed as well.

"Excellent," said Nonnie. "A contract is like a promise."

Tamika was curious. "Why do we need a contract, Nonnie?"

Nonnie smiled. "Great question. What do you think?"

Alex thought a moment, "Maybe because you want us to take this conversation* seriously?"

Nonnie nodded. "I want you to have fun while you learn, as always, but I want you to be aware of how our words matter." She paused, and then said softly. "Some people are anxious about talking openly about sexuality. I want you to understand this is an important topic."

Annie asked, "Is this why you asked my parents' permission* to talk with me?"

Nonnie said, "Yes, Annie. I want to respect your family's culture*." She opened the case she always brought to class and removed her tablet. "I have a word of my own. I'd like to share it before we start our conversation about sex."

46

Fear

Nonnie typed the word fear on the tablet. "Let's play a game," she said.

She removed sticky notes, pens, and a hat from her purse. Nonnie said, "The game is called Fear in a Hat*. Each person writes a fear on the paper without using their names. Then, we put the notes in the hat and take turns reading them. We don't read our own note." She added, smiling, "Remember, a person may pass."

Tamika, Alex and Annie wrote their notes. They placed their folded notes in the hat and picked another person's note to read. "Remember our guidelines," Nonnie reminded.

Alex read, "I'm afraid I'll never get my phone back." He looked surprised. "I didn't write this," he said, waving the note.

"I did," said Tamika. She read her note, "I'm afraid no one will ever really like me." She looked around. "I think we all could write this note."

Annie read, "I'm afraid we'll never start talking about sex." Everyone laughed.

*Nonnie learned the game Fear in a Hat from her friend Teri Shilling, nearly 20 years ago!.

AcademyPress ~ www.healthyteens.com

What Do YOU Think?

Nonnie is using games to teach.
Would you like to play
Roses and Thorns or Fear in a Hat?

Would you list a rose or a thorn from your last week?
Do you have any fears for the hat?

Please draw
or write your
thoughts
here:

AcademyPress ~ www.healthyteens.com

Nonnie said, "I think each of you can have empathy for those fears."

Alex said, "Yeah. What's your fear, Nonnie?" he asked. "You didn't write a note."

Nonnie frowned. "My fear is I won't be able to help you own the message* about respect online."

Annie looked at her, confused. "What do you mean, own the message?"

"To own a message," Nonnie said, "students must take it to heart. The message becomes part of them." She made her hands into a heart. "These words are important, aren't they? she smiled at the children and continued, "Have you thought about the word holistic?"

Alex said, "We looked it up online. Holistic means *the whole is more than the sum of the parts*." He scratched his head. "I don't know what the definition means."

Annie said, "I asked my Mom. She said holistic healthcare means a kind of medicine* where the whole person is considered in treatment." Annie's mom is a pediatrician.

 AcademyPress ~ www.healthyteens.com

Chapter Eight: The Sexual Health and Reproduction Circle

Tamika added, "My Dad said holistic is a way of looking at life. He said it means thinking of the world as all of its parts instead of only one piece, as if people are interconnected*." Tamika's father is a minister.

Nonnie was pleased. "Good research. I'm glad you looked online and also checked with trusted adults." She smiled at the children. "You're all correct. When a health care provider uses holistic medicine, the whole person is considered. Alex," she asked, "does the definition make more sense to you?"

"I guess," he said, "so, when we talk about sexuality, we don't just talk about one part of it, like having sex."

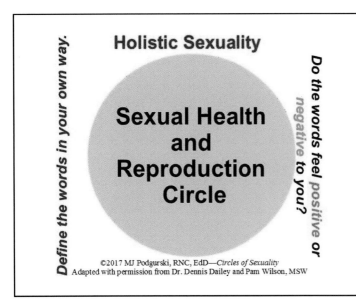

Holistic Sexuality

Define the words in your own way.

Do the words feel positive or negative to you?

Sexual Health and Reproduction Circle

©2017 MJ Podgurski, RNC, EdD—*Circles of Sexuality*
Adapted with permission from Dr. Dennis Dailey and Pam Wilson, MSW

"We talk about anything connected to sexuality," Tamika added, "right?"
"Correct," Nonnie said. "According to our contract, we start with a Circle of Sexuality, then each of you share a word you chose. Let's begin with the Sexual Health and Reproduction Circle.

50

Nonnie asked, "What do you know about sexual health and reproduction?"

Tamika was excited. "We learned about reproduction when our baby cousins were born. You taught us about birth and how babies are made, Nonnie*."

Alex smiled, "We love playing with Lily and Zion, don't we Tamika?"

Tamika laughed. "They're a lot of fun and they're messy," she said.

Annie asked, "How are babies made?"

Nonnie was pleased. Annie was feeling more comfortable!

*See *Nonnie Talks about Pregnancy and Birth* for more info.

AcademyPress ~ www.healthyteens.com

Alex asked, "Can Tamika and I be like peer educators and teach Annie?"

Nonnie thought a moment, then nodded. "Yes. I think you're ready to teach."

Tamika asked, "Can we go to the college's biology lab?"

Nonnie's friend Professor Canale welcomed them into her lab, and Alex talked with her quietly for a few minutes while Tamika took a huge biology book from the shelf.

Alex brought a slide from the Professor's collection to the microscope. "Here," he said. "Look. These tiny wiggly things are sperm*. You can only see them with a microscope. They're part of the story!"

52   AcademyPress ~ www.healthyteens.com

Tamika added, "Sperm are made in testicles*. They leave the testicles and swim out the penis*." She opened a page in the biology book. "This is fertilization*. The egg is called an ovum*. It releases from the ovary. When the sperm swim up the vagina* into the uterus* and fallopian tube*, it unites with an egg, if one is there. A baby is made!"

Nonnie was impressed. Alex and Tamika remembered a great deal about pregnancy and birth!

Annie looked confused, though. "How does the sperm get into the vagina?" she asked.

Tamika giggled, "Well! Nonnie, back to you!"

Nonnie laughed. "Thanks, Tamika." She asked Annie, "What have you heard about sex? You might have heard the word intercourse* used for sex."

Annie blushed. "On the bus...people talk about sex a lot."

Alex laughed, "No big deal, Annie. The bus ride is Sex Ed 101!"

Tamika added, "What you hear on the bus isn't always the truth!"

 AcademyPress ~ www.healthyteens.com

This is the picture from the biology book.

What Makes a Baby!

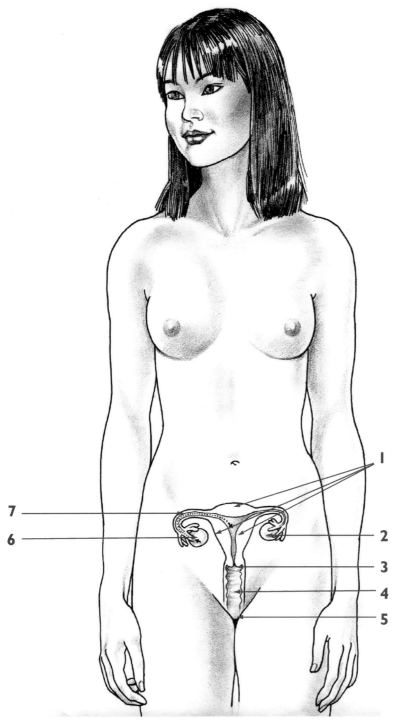

Important Stuff
1 = Uterus
2 = Ovary*
3 = Cervix*
4 = Vagina
5 = Vulva*
6 = The Ovum (Egg) is released from the Ovary
7 = The Fertilized Egg* travels through the Fallopian Tube to implant in the wall of Uterus
8 = Sperm

Fertilization happens in the Fallopian Tube when the sperm and egg unite!

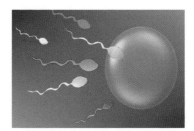

Sperm are really small! They're smaller in real life than either picture!

Nonnie explained the picture and said, "The type of sexual behavior* that makes a baby is one kind of sex. There are other types."

AcademyPress ~ www.healthyteens.com

Nonnie said, "Sexual behaviors are usually about body parts. Let's see how comfortable you are with this information."

She gave each child a sticky note and said, "Let's do a private vote. Let me know how comfortable you are talking about sex by writing a number on your note. If you're very uncomfortable, write the number 1. If you're uncomfortable, write a 2. If you're in the middle, write a 3. If you're comfortable, write a 4, and if you're very comfortable, write a 5. Put the notes in my Curiosity Bag and I'll know how you feel."

1 2 3 4 5

There were three 5's in the bag!

Tamika smiled. "I missed your Curiosity Bag, Nonnie!" she said.

Annie said, "What kind of bag?" and Alex said, "Curiosity is OK. We can write any question and put it in the bag without our names. Nonnie will answer."

WHAT DO YOU THINK?
What number would you write?
How comfortable are you talking about sex?
Are you curious about sex?

 Nonnie asked, "Do you want to write questions, or just ask them out loud?"

"Out loud," Alex and Tamika said together, and Annie nodded, agreeing. "Whatever pleases you," said Nonnie.

"You said there were different kinds of sexual behaviors Nonnie," said Tamika. Alex added quickly, "We know the kind of sex that makes babies. It involves a penis and a vagina, right?"

Annie giggled, and Nonnie said to her, "They've talked about this with me before." She turned to her grandson and his best friend Tamika, whom she loved like a granddaughter. "Yes," she said. "The kind of sexual behavior that makes babies involves the penis entering the vagina and leaving sperm there."

Annie said, "I heard about that." Alex added, "I saw a little bit of a sex video when I was in the back of the school bus. I think it was called porn*."

Nonnie said gently, "Let's talk about those kinds of videos. I'm not angry with you, Alex. Usually, the sex in pornography* isn't like sex in real life, and porn is created for adults."

56 AcademyPress ~ www.healthyteens.com

Alex said, "Everyone was watching it."

"I know," Nonnie soothed. "May I tell you a story?"

The children said, yes. They were curious about Nonnie's story.

Nonnie said, "Alex, when your Aunt Lisa was a toddler, we went to the beach. She was like a little scientist. She would walk to the ocean's edge and stand as the waves came to the shore. In a little while, a wave would knock her down. She'd pull herself back up and come to me. "Mommy," she'd say, "water moves."

"What a cute story, Nonnie," said Annie.

"What does it have to do with porn?" asked Alex.

"It is a cute story, Annie, and the memory makes me happy. I can hear the sound of the waves and watch my little one as she figures things out." Nonnie smiled. "I think of that memory to make me smile."

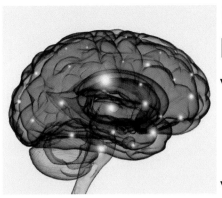

Nonnie touched her forehead. "Our brains are magic. Many memories stay with us."

Nonnie picked up her cell phone. "Alex, when children watch sexual behaviors made for adult entertainment, the memories can stay. Someday, when the children are older and want to have a sexual partner, the memories might give them the wrong idea about sex."

Tamika said, "You want us to have sex ed, though?"

"I do, Tamika," agreed Nonnie. "Quality sexuality education is medically accurate* and teaches facts. Porn is not sex ed."

"We love your sex ed classes," Alex said, "How do you know what to teach?"

"I listen to young people to find out what they need. I study and do research. I'm certified* to teach. The best teaching I do, though, is through our peer educators." Nonnie thought a minute. "Since so many young people are seeing sexual things online, I think sex ed is even more important. Confusion and myths* are common after kids see porn."

58 AcademyPress ~ www.healthyteens.com

Alex said, "I understand. I have questions, too. I'm not going to watch that stuff again, no matter who shows it on the bus."

Nonnie smiled, "You're not an adult, Alex, so good. Ask me your questions. You won't get in trouble."

Alex hesitated, so Tamika started talking. "I know there are other kinds of sex, too, Nonnie."

"So do I," said Annie. "So does everyone I know."

"My question is about oral sex*," Tamika said. She wanted to help Alex feel safe. She also was interested in answers to her questions. "Do people really do that?"

Nonnie said, "Yes. Oral sex is placing mouth to genitals. Genitals* is the fancy word for sexual body parts."

Alex said, "What people call junk*!"

Everyone laughed, and Nonnie said, "People certainly make up funny names for body parts. Genitals are important, though, Alex—they're not garbage!"

AcademyPress ~ www.healthyteens.com

"Babies don't happen from oral sex, right?" asked Alex. "Or, from any other sexual behavior except the one we talked about. Right?

"Correct," said Nonnie. "There needs to be sperm, an egg, and a uterus to start a pregnancy. A baby needs to grow inside a uterus. A pregnancy cannot occur from a mouth and genitals."

She watched the children closely. They still seemed curious, so she asked, "What else do you want to know?"

"Is kissing sexual behavior?" Annie asked.

"What do you think?" asked Nonnie. Annie said, "Maybe."

Tamika said, "Not a kiss on the check, like I give Lily and Zion when we see them."

"Right. Kissing on the mouth is different." Annie giggled, and covered her own mouth "I've never kissed anyone like that, but I see it in movies all the time."

Tamika snorted. "I told my Mom it looks like couples kissing on TV are trying to chew each other's mouths! I've seen people kissing. It's not like in the movies."

60 AcademyPress ~ www.healthyteens.com

Alex started laughing at the idea of his parents kissing like people kissed in movies. Soon he was laughing loudly!

Nonnie watched him closely. She knew people may laugh when they are embarrassed or anxious. She waited for Alex's next questions.

Alex said, "I think kissing is one kind of sexual behavior. Another sexual behavior is touching someone else's body. Touching yourself sexually is called masturbation* or self-pleasuring*." He glanced at Nonnie and said, "I read that."

Tamika said, "It's OK to touch your own body, but you need to get consent* to touch someone else's body." Nonnie agreed.

She asked Nonnie for her tablet and wrote on it. "This is my word for today," she said. "If sending nude pics is sexual, I think people need to get consent."

Consent

Annie said, "Consent means saying 'yes,' correct?"

Alex said, "Yep. My aunt teaches me to stop tickling Lily if she says 'no,' even if she's laughing. Aunt Tracy says we're teaching Lily consent."

61

 AcademyPress ~ www.healthyteens.com

Annie looked sad. She said, "Ethan didn't ask me if he could share my pic. I wish I never sent it to him!" She took the tablet from Tamika and wrote her word. "I feel confused*," she said. "How could I like him so much? He must not like me at all."

Confused

Alex shook his head. "I think Ethan is confused, too, Annie. He didn't respect you, but that doesn't mean he didn't like you." He frowned. "Guys are complicated," he moaned.

"All people are complicated," Nonnie corrected.

Privacy

Alex frowned and wrote on the tablet. When he stepped back, they saw the word privacy.* He turned to Annie. "I didn't know you very well when this happened. Now, you're my friend, and I'm sorry I didn't protect your privacy."

Annie thanked him, then said sadly, "As soon as I sent the pic, I gave up my privacy. What a dumb move."

Nonnie said, "Remember, honey, Ethan violated your trust. You made a decision you would probably change, you wish you could take it back, and you didn't think he would share it. Sharing the pic wasn't OK."

       AcademyPress ~ www.healthyteens.com

Tamika said, "I guess once we send something online we lose control of it." She looked at the Circle on the card and asked, "I think we learned some of these topics in health class."

"I'm sure you did, honey," Nonnie sighed. "A lot of sex ed is about preventing teen pregnancy* and STI*s. Those are important topics, but they're not the only concepts I teach."

Prevention

"What else is important, Nonnie?" Alex asked.

Nonnie said, "Over time, I learned young people need help with relationships* and sexual health*. I do teach about preventing early childbearing and STIs, but I make sure my messages are about developing as healthy people, too."

Annie wrinkled her nose. "I hate health class. All those gross pictures of infections. Ugh."

Nonnie smiled. "I don't show those kinds of pictures, but it is important to learn about STIs like gonorrhea* and herpes*. I'm especially concerned about silent infections, like HPV* (human papillomavirus) or chlamydia* or HIV*, where many people do not know they are infected. I do teach about sexually transmitted infections (STIs)."

63

Annie said, "My Mom made me get a vaccine for HPV. She said it helps prevent cancer." She rubbed her arm. "It's tough when you're mom is a pediatrician!"

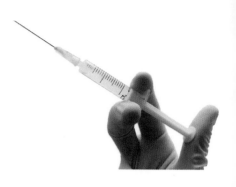

"I got one," said Tamika. "Me, too," added Alex.

Nonnie smiled. "Prevention* is important. In the 1980s, I was able to start teaching sex ed in some of our schools because people were concerned about HIV* and AIDS*.

Alex said, "I already know this! I've heard about bacteria and viruses."

"You might, Alex!" Nonnie said, "I think knowing the difference between a bacterial infection and a viral one is a first step, but the key message I want you to know is how to prevent infection."

"An infection caused by a bacteria can be treated with drugs, right?" Tamika asked.

"Yes," said Nonnie. "Antibiotics treat bacterial infections like gonorrhea, chlamydia and syphilis* by killing the bacteria. A viral infection is different, but the symptoms* can be treated. Antiviral medications can help."

Alex asked, "Maybe I do need more information. How can we prevent STIs or HIV?"

Nonnie said, "Knowing your partner is important. People need to talk openly about past sexual histories. Prevention, or using a barrier method of protection, like a condom*, is also key. There are even special medicines adults can take to keep from getting infected with HIV."

Annie said, "My teacher said condoms don't stop STIs."

Nonnie said, "Some STIs, like herpes and HPV, can be spread by skin to skin contact, which means they might still be spread, even if a person uses a condom. Research* is very clear, however. Using a condom lowers risk of infection—it is the best protection if people decide to have sex."

"What about teen pregnancy?" asked Alex. "I know you help young parents."

Nonnie said, "I started volunteering with young parents in the 1970s, Alex. I respect them and try to empower them."

"I'm way too young to be a parent," said Tamika firmly. "My Mom talks with me."
"So am I," added Alex. "I'm still a kid!"

 AcademyPress ~ www.healthyteens.com

Annie said, "My Mom talks with me, too. I think I'm too young for sex."

Nonnie said, "I'm glad you all talk with parents. We don't always know a person's story. People have sex for many reasons. Not all young parents agreed to intercourse."

The children were quiet. Tamika said, "We shouldn't judge."

Alex agreed, then said, "My Dad says, as soon as sex happens, life can get more complicated."

"How?" asked Annie.

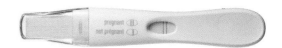

"Like, if there's an unplanned pregnancy," said Alex. "Dad says even some babies born to adults are surprises!"

"I think deciding to use contraception*, and what method to use, is a big deal," said Tamika. She smiled. "Between my Mom and my Aunt Janell, I know all kinds of things about birth control."

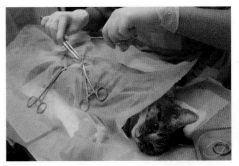

She shook her head. "My cat needed surgery when I was little. Since then, I've wanted to be a vet and fix animals. I'll need lots of years in school. I need to study!"

Nonnie said, "Setting goals* in life is so very important. Remember, there's more to sexuality than having sex."

66

Annie looked at Nonnie's Circles card game.

"Menopause!" Annie laughed. "My Mom says she's feels hot all the time because of it."

Nonnie said, "Some people do feel hot during menopause, which is the end of fertility* for females. Males and females feel changes in the middle of the life-span*."

Tamika asked, "Do periods stop then?"

Nonnie said, "Yes," which made Tamika laugh. "I really don't like periods. It makes so little sense to have them when the last thing I want to do right now is make a baby."

Annie looked like she was thinking. Her face was pinched, as if she was worried. Nonnie said, "What's on your mind, Annie?"

"It doesn't seem fair," Annie said. "My Mom has a friend who wants a baby but can't get pregnant. What is that called?"

"Infertility*," said Nonnie. "There are fertility clinics where people can get help for infertility, though."

67

"My Mom also has a friend who got pregnant after she was raped in college. She ended the pregnancy with an abortion*." Annie shook her head. "I wish all of this was easier."

Alex said, "My dad is always talking with me about consent. I guess he's not just nagging me."

Nonnie shook her head, "Not at all, Alex. He wants to teach you. There are serious legal consequences if someone has sex with a person without consent." She turned to Annie and said, "I'm glad your mom talks openly with you."

Alex glanced at the cards, "I don't like to think about sexual dysfunction* or impotence*. I'd like to think the body works without any problems."

Tamika snorted. "I thought I was the one who liked to watch romantic comedies, where everything works out perfectly. You always laugh and call them chick flicks. Real life is more messy, right Nonnie?"

"It can be," said Nonnie. "Bodies don't always work, but relationships can be healthy and meaningful, even when there are challenges. Do you have any questions?"

AcademyPress ~ www.healthyteens.com

"Can you list the topics?" Alex was curious. "I'd like to see what we've learned in this Circle."

Nonnie wrote in red on a yellow poster. "This Circle covers a lot of challenging topics. Some are easy to talk about and some are difficult. Please talk about what you've learned with your parents. Here are some of the topics in the Sexual Health and Reproduction Circle:"

♦ Abortion (ending a pregnancy)

♦ Anatomy and Physiology of Body Parts (what each part is and how it works)

♦ Contraception (preventing a pregnancy)

♦ Impotence (trouble having an erection*)

♦ Infertility (trouble making a baby)

♦ Menopause (when an ovary stops releasing eggs)

♦ Sexual Behaviors (what people do sexually)

♦ Sexual Dysfunction (when people have sexual problems)

♦ STIs (infections spread through sexual contact— called sexually transmitted infections)

 AcademyPress ~ www.healthyteens.com

What Do YOU Think?

Nonnie's correct. The topics in the Sexual Health and Reproduction Circle are complicated.

Which topics in the Circle are easy for you to discuss? Which topics are difficult for you?

Please draw or write your thoughts here:

70

AcademyPress ~ www.healthyteens.com

Nonnie said, "If you're curious about any of the topics, I'll answer your questions. For now, I think this is enough for one day." She sighed. "I also think I need a nap."

They walked by the college library on their way home. A student was sleeping at his desk. Tamika pointed and said, "Nonnie, you're not the only one who needs a nap."

Annie said, "Nap time should be part of everyone's day!"

The week passed quickly this time. It was testing week at school, Annie and Alex attended Tamika's soccer game, and they all went to the movies together. Annie was happier.

Their next meeting happened at Tamika's grandmother's townhouse in an assisted living facility* for elderly people. Since her grandfather's death*, Tamika spends as much time as possible with her grandma. Her name is Emilea. Tamika calls her abuelita* and gave her a big hug.

*See *Nonnie Talks about Death* for more info.

     AcademyPress ~ www.healthyteens.com

Chapter Nine: The Sensuality Circle

The children swam in the pool while the grandmas drank tea.

After swimming, Tamika, Alex and Annie gathered around Nonnie and Tamika's abuelita. Nonnie said, "We're going to help you understand another Circle of Sexuality together. The Circle is the Sensuality Circle."

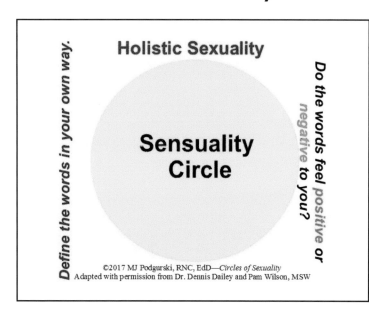

Holistic Sexuality

Define the words in your own way.

Do the words feel positive or negative to you?

Sensuality Circle

©2017 MJ Podgurski, RNC, EdD—*Circles of Sexuality*
Adapted with permission from Dr. Dennis Dailey and Pam Wilson, MSW

Annie said, "Sensuality. Does the word come from our senses, like hearing, seeing, and touching?"

"Excellent, Annie!" Nonnie beamed at her. "You are exactly right. Sensuality is about an experience that is pleasing to the senses."

Tamika's abuelita went into her kitchen and returned with five tall glasses of Refresco de Papaya, a papaya and milk smoothie from her homeland, the Dominican Republic. Emilea said, "This will please your sense of taste."

72

Everyone enjoyed the drink!

Nonnie said, "I'd like to teach an important part of the Sensuality Circle. You may think the words are strange. What do you think skin hunger means?"

Alex laughed. "People eating other people's skin?"

Tamika said, "Nope. I'm sure skin hunger means something else."

"It does," Nonnie said. "Human beings need touch to feel OK. If no one touches an infant, the baby will not grow well and be healthy."

Emilea added, "If an elderly person is never touched, except for medical treatments, the person may become sad." She reached over and hugged Tamika again. "My grandchildren make sure I get plenty of hugs and touch."

Alex said, "So sad, Nonnie." He gave her a big hug, too. "I promise, you won't ever be without my hugs."

Both grandmas felt very lucky and very loved!

73 AcademyPress ~ www.healthyteens.com

Annie was interested. "What else is in the Sensuality Circle?" she asked.

Nonnie said, "I wonder if you can guess." Tamika said, "Chocolate!" Emilea laughed, and agreed with her grandchild. Chocolate was pleasant. "Some people say certain foods make a person feel sexy," Nonnie shrugged, "like oysters." "Ewwww," said Alex.

Annie asked, "What about the other senses? How does hearing fit into the Circle?"

Alex said, "Let me guess. If you hear romantic music, it may make you feel loving. Couples often talk about hearing 'their song!'"

"Yes," said Nonnie. "How about smell?"

"Are perfumes and colognes sensuous?" asked Tamika. "Yes," said Nonnie. "And, each person has a special odor."

"Weird," said Annie.

Alex laughed. "It is, but I believe it's true. When I don't see my mom for a while, she holds me tight. I swear she's smelling my hair."

74 AcademyPress ~ www.healthyteens.com

Annie asked, "What about sight?"

Alex was quiet. Tamika thought she knew why. He said, "When someone watches something sexual, Nonnie, does it fit in this circle?"

 Why do you think Alex was quiet?

Nonnie said, "Yes. Pleasure can come from something one sees. Viewing paintings or sculptures showing the human body as a beautiful work of art can be sensuous."

Tamika said, "We saw a picture of Michelangelo's David* in Social Studies. Some kids laughed."

Her abuelita said, "There are always people who don't understand the beauty of the human body. It is their loss."

Nonnie said, "Another part of the Sensuality Circle is body image*. What do those words mean to you?"
"How we see ourselves," said Tamika.

"Correct. Why is body image connected to sexuality?" Emilea asked her granddaughter.

75

"Maybe," Tamika said, "if we don't like our bodies and don't think they are worthy*, we might not connect well with others."

Annie looked uncomfortable. She squirmed in her seat, then suddenly stood up, looking out the window.

Nonnie looked at her. "Do you want to talk about something, honey?" she asked kindly.

Annie turned to them. "I just realized. I was so unhappy with my own body that I did something weird. I tried to change it with an online picture."

Tamika moved to stand beside her. "We all make mistakes, remember?"

Annie sighed. "Why didn't I like my body as it was?"

Alex stood and went to stand by his friends. "I think most of us want to change our bodies right now. Being in 6th grade can be strange!"

76 AcademyPress ~ www.healthyteens.com

Nonnie said, "How strong you three are together! Yes, Annie, I think your body image wasn't positive then. You're growing and changing. How do you feel about your body now?

Annie was quiet a moment, then she smiled. "I like it more." Tamika hugged her, and Alex gave her a high five.

Emilea said, "Positive body image is important. Nonnie, you've done a great job teaching these children."

Nonnie smiled. "Gracias*," she said, "they are very wise. They teach themselves, each other, and me. Which reminds me," she turned to the children. "What are your words for today?"

Tamika said, "My word is friendship." She smiled, looking at her friends. Annie looked very happy.

"Friendship is an important take home message from our time together," Nonnie said.

Alex said, "My word is kind of like Tamika's word. I picked the word human*. I think we need to consider what other humans need. We all want to be treated with respect and dignity."

77

Before Nonnie could say anything, Annie added, "My word this week is encouragement*. You've really encouraged me."

Nonnie liked the children's words. Alex asked, "Do you have a word this week, Nonnie?"

She said, "My word this week is pleasure*. What do you think it means?"

"Something that makes a person feel happy?" asked Annie.

"Since we're talking about sexuality, could it be about sexual pleasure?" asked Tamika. She turned to her abuelita. "What does sexual pleasure feel like?"

Emelia said, "I'm so glad you asked me, Tamika. No one ever explained anything sexual to me when I was a girl. One's body reacts with a good feeling when sexually excited. This can happen alone or with a partner."

"What do you call this feeling?" asked Annie.

Nonnie said, "Many people call the feeling of sexual pleasure an orgasm*, but a person doesn't need to have an orgasm to feel pleasure. People learn their own bodies and what feels good to them."

78

"Do only men have orgasms, Nonnie," asked Annie.

"No," said Nonnie. "Any person may have an orgasm or sexual pleasure."

Alex said. "Are there other topics in the Sensuality Circle?"

Nonnie said, "Yes. What do you think the word fantasy* means?"

Tamika said, "Sexy things you think about? Maybe, a celebrity you're crushing on. Or," Tamika glanced at her abuelita, "a crush in real life."

Alex said, "Don't people sell novels to encourage fantasy?"

Tamika snorted, "To encourage people to buy books, you mean?"

Her abuelita laughed. "I have friends who love romance novels. They enjoy sexy thoughts."

Annie asked, "Are those thoughts OK?"

AcademyPress ~ www.healthyteens.com

"Thoughts are OK, but some books are too intense for a young person," said Nonnie. "A young person may need a trusted adult to help sort out their thoughts."

Emilea asked Tamika, "Do you want to talk about a crush?" Tamika giggled. "Not today, abuelita," she said. "Maybe the next time I come to visit."

Nonnie said, "Here are the Sensuality Circle topics:"

- Body Image (how we see our bodies)

- Fantasy (what we imagine or think about)

- Human Sexual Response Cycle (how bodies reach orgasm)

- Pleasure (a good feeling)

- Sight (what we see)

- Skin Hunger (the need for touch)

- Smell (pleasing odors)

- Sound (what we hear)

- Taste (pleasing things to eat)

- Touch (contact with another person)

80

 AcademyPress ~ www.healthyteens.com

What Do YOU Think?

The topics in the Sensuality Circle
may seem strange to you.

Which topics in this circle are easy for you to discuss?
Which topics are difficult for you?
Do you think this circle is named well? Why or why not?

Please draw
or write your
thoughts
here:

AcademyPress ~ www.healthyteens.com

Chapter Ten: The Sexual Identity Circle

Alex said, "Can we talk about the next Circle today? I don't want to wait."

Nonnie looked at her watch. "If it's OK with you, Emilea?" Tamika's abuelita agreed. She enjoyed talking with the children and Nonnie.

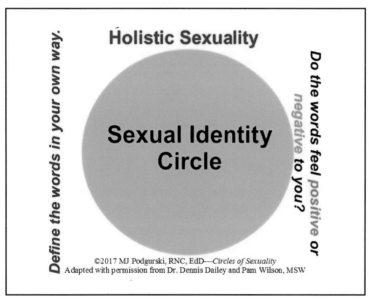

"The next Circle of Sexuality is the Sexual Identity Circle," Nonnie said. "Can anyone tell me what the word identity* means?"

"Who we are?" guessed Tamika.

"How we see ourselves," said Annie, "or who we want to be."

"How other people see us," said Alex. "We could search the definition, if we had our phones." He sounded sad and wistful and annoyed, all at once.

Nonnie handed him her cell. Alex grinned and immediately began searching the word identity.

82

Tamika and Annie leaned over Alex's shoulder to watch him. Tamika sighed. "I miss my phone," she whispered. Alex shared the phone, and Tamika looked happy.

In a few minutes, Alex said, "We were right." Tamika added, "Identity is who or what a person or thing is."

"What does sexual identity cover?" Annie asked, curious.

Nonnie said, "This circle contains a person's biological sex and gender. It includes gender identity, gender roles, and sexual orientation."

Tamika and Alex looked at each other. "Nonnie taught us about gender when we were younger. Our friend Avian transitioned to his true self a year ago, during puberty."

Annie was confused. "Transitioned? True self? Biological sex? Gender? Help!"

 AcademyPress ~ www.healthyteens.com

Alex grinned. "Our turn to teach again, Nonnie?"

Nonnie laughed and said, "Go for it." She turned to Emilea, "Maybe I will retire one day!"

Tamika said, "I wish we had something to write on."
In minutes, Emilea had them inside her townhouse, in front of a large whiteboard. She handed Tamika markers, and Tamika gave her a kiss on the cheek. "I forgot about these. You bought them for me when my abuelito was sick. He liked to draw for me, and we played games together."

Tamika was sad. Alex hugged her. So did Nonnie. Then she took a big breath. "Let's teach, Alex," she said.

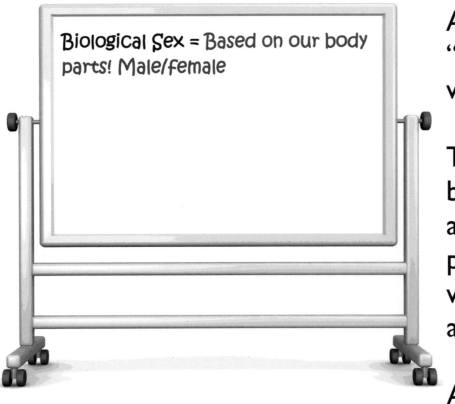

Biological Sex = Based on our body parts! Male/female

Alex said, "More important words!"

Tamika said, "Your biological sex is about the body parts you're born with...like a penis or a vulva."

Annie said, "OK."

84 AcademyPress ~ www.healthyteens.com

Nonnie added the word intersex* to the board.

Tamika said, "The word intersex is new to me."

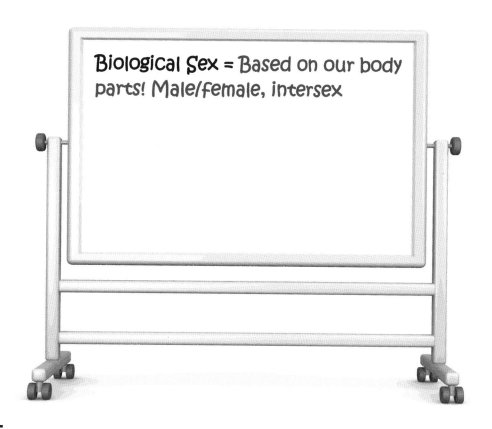

Emilea said, "I have a cousin who is intersex. She identifies as a woman now, but at birth was born with both male and female genitals."

Alex was interested. "I think parents would worry when a baby is born intersex."

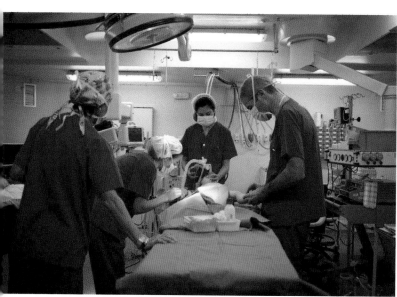

Nonnie smiled at Alex. "At first, Alex. Parents want life to be easy for their babies. An intersex baby can have a great life. When I was a young nurse, doctors would make a decision about an intersex person's gender when the person was a baby. Often, surgery was done to remove genitals."

85

Annie said, "That doesn't seem fair. What happens to intersex babies now?"

Biological Sex = Based on our body parts! Male/female, intersex
Gender = Girl/boy, non-binary gender

Nonnie said, "Some healthcare providers wait to see how the child develops and identifies. I like that approach*."

Tamika added the word gender to the board. She said, "Your gender is shaped by your society*. Some societies believe there are two genders, men and women—that's called binary* gender. Other societies, like some Native peoples, have more than two genders.

Annie asked, "Does everyone in our society identify as binary– with two genders?"

Alex said, "No. People may identify as gender-fluid* or non-binary*."

AcademyPress ~ www.healthyteens.com

"Our friend Avian identifies as a boy, but his sex assigned at birth was female," added Alex. He wrote gender identity on the board.

Biological Sex = Based on our body parts! Male/female, intersex
Gender = Girl/boy, non-binary gender
Gender Identity = Our identity is who we are, regardless of biology

Emilea said, "One of my childhood friends has a granddaughter who identifies as transgender*. Her sex assigned at birth was male, but she identifies as a girl."

Annie said, "Her true self."

"Right, Annie," said Alex.

"When a person's body parts match their gender identity, they are called cisgender*," added Tamika.

Annie said, "I've heard about this on the news, but no one ever explained things to me. I was always curious."

Tamika added, "People our age need honest answers!"

87 AcademyPress ~ www.healthyteens.com

Annie frowned. "I don't think my dad would like some of these topics."

Nonnie spoke gently. "We respect all people's opinions*, including your Dad's. I think we can probably agree each person is worthy of respect. A person doesn't need to understand or even accept difference to honor another human's dignity."

Annie nodded, then asked, "What are gender roles? I've also heard about gender expression. What's that?"

Alex asked, "Can you guess?"
Tamika said, "Two questions. Which one first?"

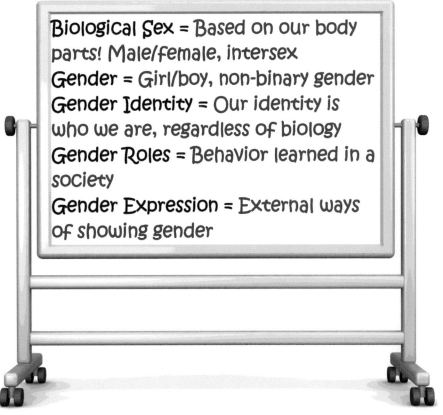

Biological Sex = Based on our body parts! Male/female, intersex
Gender = Girl/boy, non-binary gender
Gender Identity = Our identity is who we are, regardless of biology
Gender Roles = Behavior learned in a society
Gender Expression = External ways of showing gender

Annie thought a bit. "I think gender expression is the way we dress or show our gender?"

Alex said, "Yes," then asked, "Don't we learn the behavior for gender roles as we grow up?"

"Totally!" Tamika said.

88 AcademyPress ~ www.healthyteens.com

She added, "A society teaches gender roles, maybe without words. Toy stores have aisles and aisles of "boy toys" and "girl toys" for sale. Kids just like to play."

"I get it," said Annie. "What does sexual orientation mean?"

Nonnie said, "Do you remember when we mentioned attraction and lust?"

Alex grinned. "Lust was going to be my word for this circle!"

"Attraction is about who looks good to a person, or who a person is drawn to emotionally. Emotions are feelings. Attraction may lead to sexual desire. Lust is strong sexual desire," Nonnie said.

89 AcademyPress ~ www.healthyteens.com

She turned to Emilea. "Do you have a TV I can use?"

Emilea was happy to help. Nonnie pulled a jump drive from her purse. Nonnie said, "I use these pictures of real people to teach about attraction and sexual orientation in my college class."

A person may be attracted to men or women or both," said Nonnie. Annie said, "My uncle Sam is gay. I love him, but our family doesn't talk about him much."

Alex frowned. "He is worthy of respect," he said.

Tamika said, "Is he a good person, Annie?"

Annie said, "Yes, a very good person. He teaches kids with disabilities."

 AcademyPress ~ www.healthyteens.com

The children were sad, and then Tamika said, "I have an online friend who says she is pansexual*. I haven't texted with her since my phone was taken away. What does pan-sexual mean?"

Nonnie said, "A person who identifies as pansexual doesn't limit partners based on gender or gender identity or biological sex. Pan is Greek for all." She smiled at Tamika. "People are unique*. Each person is different from each other person. It's not necessary to understand another person's identity. It's enough to respect the person and treat everyone with dignity."

Tamika said, "Since we didn't bring a word for this Circle of Sexuality, Nonnie, may I use unique as my word today? I like the idea of each person being different." Emilea smiled. "I like being your abuelita, Tamika. Your abuelito would be proud of the person you are."

Annie asked, "What can be my word for this Circle?"

Nonnie said, "Think a bit. What comes to your mind?" Annie was quiet. She asked, "What word means a place where people belong?" "Maybe society," said Tamika. She thought of what she might find if she searched online for the word society.

 AcademyPress ~ www.healthyteens.com

"Not exactly what I'm looking for, though," said Annie. She grinned at Nonnie. "Words matter," she said. "I want to find the correct one."

Suddenly, Annie clapped her hands. "I have it! Community*. My word for the Circle of Sexual Identity is community. A community can exist online or in real life or both."

"I like it," said Alex. "It's the best word yet."

"We're a community," Tamika said, agreeing. She made a huge circle with her hands and pretended to draw everyone together. "We support each other."

92

"We are a community, Tamika," Nonnie said, and Tamika's abuelita smiled, agreeing.

Alex added, "People who are heterosexual, or straight, are attracted to another sex, right Nonnie? Most people are straight."

"Correct, Alex," Nonnie said.

"If a person isn't straight, do they have a community for support?" Annie asked.

"Yes," Nonnie smiled. "In our town, we host a GSA, a gay-straight alliance. Teens attend if they identify as LGBTQAI (lesbian*, gay*, bisexual*, trans, questioning*, asexual*, or intersex), or if they are allies*. Allies support others, but do not speak for the group they support."

93

"What's asexual, Nonnie?" asked Annie.

Nonnie said, "An asexual person may not be interested in physical sex. The kind of touching that makes a person feel sexy may be unwanted or unpleasant for some people."

Emilea added, "I was a social worker before I retired. I knew people who felt they were asexual, but loved to cuddle or hold hands. Nonnie is right, every person is different."

Nonnie agreed. "A person may be asexual but romantic. Romance means the person may like to go on dates or pay attention to another person in other ways."

Tamika said, "My word. Unique."

Nonnie said, "I know. Each person is a person of worth."

 AcademyPress ~ www.healthyteens.com

Alex said, "I thought I knew everything about this Circle, but I learned a lot!"

"So did I," said Tamika.

Annie said, "So many of my questions were answered, before I even asked them."

"Do you have another word for today, Nonnie, since we talked about two Circles?" Tamika was curious.

"I do," Nonnie said, "My second word is gratitude*." She thanked Emilea. "I liked sharing today with all of you. Here are the topics in the Sexual Identity Circle:"

♦ Biological Sex (our body parts; male/female; intersex)

♦ Gender (girl/boy or non-binary, based on society)

♦ Gender Identity (the way a person sees self based on gender)

♦ Gender Roles (the way a culture or society expects people to act, based on their gender)

♦ Sexual Orientation (who one is attracted to, emotionally and/or physically)

95

What Do YOU Think?

Some people might find the topics in the Sexual Identity Circle controversial*.
What does controversial mean?
Do you think these topics should be controversial?
Are they complicated? What do the topics mean to you?

Please draw or write your thoughts here:

AcademyPress ~ www.healthyteens.com

Something wonderful happened during the next week. Alex's parents and Tamika's parents gave them back their phones!

Annie's mom wasn't ready to trust her yet.

When the children met Nonnie again, trust was the first thing on Annie's mind. It was her word for the day.

Annie was unhappy. "How can I get back my parents' trust?" she asked, sadly.

Nonnie said, "Trust can be hard to regain." She looked at Tamika and Alex. "What did you two do to restore trust in your families?"

Tamika said, "I showed I could be trusted by doing whatever I was told."

Alex said, "Not me." He grinned. "I talked about all of our lessons and the Circles of Sexuality with my parents. They were interested. They said I was learning respect." He looked proud.

Tamika added, "It helps to not be moody. I've learned to say when I've had a bad day and need time alone."

97 AcademyPress ~ www.healthyteens.com

Chapter Eleven: The Sexualization Circle

Nonnie said, "Any suggestions for Annie?"

Annie said, "I have one. Could my mom talk with you, Nonnie?" Nonnie said, "Absolutely. I'll call her tonight." She smiled at Annie and added. "Shall we look at the next Circle of Sexuality? I need to warn you...this Circle can be difficult to discuss. It's called the Sexualization Circle."

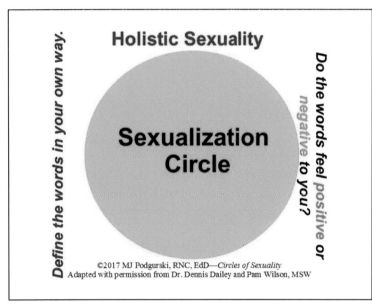

Holistic Sexuality

Sexualization Circle

Define the words in your own way.

Do the words feel positive or negative to you?

©2017 MJ Podgurski, RNC, EdD—*Circles of Sexuality*
Adapted with permission from Dr. Dennis Dailey and Pam Wilson, MSW

Tamika said, "I'm glad we didn't start with this Circle!"

Nonnie asked, "Would you like to begin with your words? We already know Annie's word is trust."

Alex said, "I love my word. It's a big one. I picked the word integrity* this week."

"What a great word, Alex!" Nonnie said. "What does it mean to you?"

"I looked it up online," Alex said with pride. "It means to be honest and to have high moral principles."

Annie asked, "What are moral principles*? I know what being honest means."

Nonnie asked. "Any idea what moral principles are?"

Tamika smiled, remembering, "My abuelito taught me about having a moral compass*. He said it was knowing right from wrong and being strong enough to do the right thing."

Nonnie remembered Tamika's grandpa well. "He was a strong man, honey."

"He dealt with a lot of racism* in his life, too*," Tamika said. "He moved to the United States and learned English when he was a boy. He was a Marine. My mom tells me he was a role model* in her life." Tamika paused. "In my life, too."

"I think he was," Alex said, "in mine, too."

The children were quiet, thinking of Tamika's abuelito and his life. "Grief* is weird, isn't it?" Tamika said, smiling sadly. "I love remembering him, but I miss him."

*See *Nonnie Talks about Race* for more info.

"We're serious today," said Annie. "Is this Circle of Sexuality serious?"

"In some ways, it is," Nonnie said. "My word for today is ethics*. It goes nicely with Alex's word."

"How, Nonnie?" asked Alex.

"Ethics are the moral principles that guide a person's behavior," Nonnie said. "Let's talk about the Sexualization Circle. We can add Tamika's word first, if you wish."

Tamika frowned. "I've put a lot of thought into my word this time. I picked legal*."

Alex stared at her. "Why, Tamika?"

 Tamika shook her head. "I just think we need to remember that sending nude pics of underage people is not legal in most states." She paused. "Should it be illegal?"

Nonnie asked, "What do you think?"

Annie spoke up quickly. "I think what I did was a dumb move. My grandpa calls dumb moves 'bonehead' things people do. I don't think it makes me a sexual predator*."

100 AcademyPress ~ www.healthyteens.com

Nonnie asked the children, "Do you know what the words sexual predator mean?"

Alex said, "I think it's someone who abuses a child."

Tamika said, "Sexually."

Annie said, "When I think of the word predator, I picture an adult, not a young person."

Alex added, "So do I, Annie. The law is still the law, though. Nonnie," he said, "even if we disagree with a law or think it needs changed, don't we still need to obey it?"

Nonnie said, "Yes, we do. Schools are very firm about reporting nude pics. The law requires they make a report."

The children all moaned. "We know," said Tamika.

"What do you think your grandfather would say about this Tamika?" Nonnie asked.

Tamika thought a moment, then said, "I think he would say I should do the right thing because it was the right thing, not just because I was afraid I'd get in trouble."

101 AcademyPress ~ www.healthyteens.com

"What is this Circle about, Nonnie?" Annie asked.

Nonnie said.,"A lot in the Sexualization Circle is negative. It's about using sexuality to control* others."

"How does sexualization control others?" Tamika asked.

"One of the ways you may already know is advertising*," Nonnie said. "Ads try to get people to buy things or do something, and they often use sex to influence* people."

They were meeting at Nonnie's house, so she brought out a bag of magazines."Let's see if you can pick out some advertisements* that use sex to sell a product*."

AcademyPress ~ www.healthyteens.com

"What do you notice?" asked Nonnie.

"The men are all buff and the women are all thin," said Alex.

Annie added, "Look. This ad is selling soda but it shows two people in bed. It's using sex to sell soda!"

Tamika said, "I never thought of the way ads use sex to sell things! What else is in the Sexualization Circle, Nonnie?"

"An idea that might surprise you," said Nonnie. "Flirting*."

"How is flirting a way of using people?" Alex asked.

Nonnie said, "Imagine an event where people are getting to know one another. People feel a little awkward. Someone who is flirting can act as if there's a lot of interest in another person...as if attraction is real. Flirting may be a way to get someone to think they are liked." The children all grew quiet.

Nonnie noticed how tense they were. She remembered Alex's father talking about the first school dance for sixth graders. When his dad asked Alex what happened at the dance, he said, "Nothing"...and *nothing* was usually young person code for "I don't want to talk about it."

In fact, the children were all remembering the dance.

Suddenly, Annie said, "Ethan was flirting with me at the dance! I had no idea!"

Nonnie asked, "Did this happen before he texted you for a nude pic?"

Annie nodded. More and more, Nonnie understood why Annie sent the pic.

1. She felt alone, as if she had no friends.
2. She wanted someone to like her.
3. Ethan acted as if he did like her.

 AcademyPress ~ www.healthyteens.com

Tamika said, "I don't know exactly how you feel, Annie, but I'm so glad you shared with us."

Annie smiled. She felt safe with her friends and Nonnie.

The children were quiet a while, then Alex said, "I'm guessing the other topics in the Sexualization Circle are difficult."

"In some ways, Alex," Nonnie said.
"I want to learn about them anyway, Nonnie," Annie said with courage. Nonnie told her how brave she was, and Annie looked very proud.

"The next topics are about sexual assault. Do you think it is important to talk about these difficult topics?"

The children all said "yes" at one time!

"Why?" asked Nonnie.

"So we can support each other," said Tamika. "And learn," said Annie. Alex agreed.

 AcademyPress ~ www.healthyteens.com

Consent

Alex said, "My dad taught me it's never OK to do anything sexual without consent."

"I want to remind you of something very important," Nonnie said. "If someone hurts another person sexually, or makes the person do sexual things they don't want to do, it is never the fault of the person who is forced. Never. Even if the sexual things feel good."

Annie said, "My mom talks about this. She sometimes works with children who are abuse victims."

"Words matter, Annie." Nonnie asked the children, "Can you think of a word we can use instead of victim? A word to describe how strong a person is when they survive something difficult, like a sexual assault."

"Survivor?" Annie said, "I've heard my mom say it."
"I like it," said Tamika.

Nonnie looked sad. "I love working with children and teaching young people as they grow. The most difficult work I've ever done is with young survivors."

 AcademyPress ~ www.healthyteens.com

"Why would someone hurt a child, especially sexually?" asked Tamika.

"I don't know, Tamika," Nonnie said. "Sex is an adult activity. Little people's bodies belong to them."

Alex added, "Everyone's bodies are their own. My dad and I talk about rape whenever it gets reported on the news. He says I'm old enough to know it happens." Alex took a deep breath. "Nonnie," he said, "I have a really tough question."

"I'm here," said Nonnie, leaning towards her grandson.

"Who can be raped? Only girls and women?" Alex looked very serious, which was not his usual way to act.

"Anyone can be sexually assaulted, Alex," Nonnie said. "No matter a person's body, gender or gender identity."

The children were quiet. Nonnie waited until she thought they were OK, then she said, "Remember, no matter how old you are, there are trusted people in your lives who will listen to you. Always."

107

Tamika looked at the Circle. "I've been listening to the news. Is sexual harassment in this Circle?"

"Yes," said Nonnie, looking sad and angry at the same time.

Alex searched on his phone. "Sexual harassment," he read, "usually happens to women in the workplace, but can occur to anyone when sexual advances, touch, or language are unwanted." He looked up. "There's no respect in this type of behavior," he said, looking sad and angry at the same time, just like Nonnie.

"You're correct, Alex," Nonnie sighed. "However, sexual harassment can happen outside of the workplace, even on the street or in a public place. Many times people are afraid to tell the truth. Can you guess why?"

Annie said, "They might be afraid they'll lose their jobs."

Tamika said, "They might be worried they won't be believed."

Alex asked, "Does this happen to young people, too?"

108 AcademyPress ~ www.healthyteens.com

Nonnie said, "It can. Sexual harassment can happen at schools or youth groups. I believe education can help teach young people to honor their own bodies and to tell a trusted adult if they're treated badly."

Tamika stood up. She moved both hands in a circle over her body, from her head to her feet. "This is my body," she said. "It belongs to me."

Annie said, "Now I really get why sending the pic to Ethan wasn't OK. I didn't understand until our talks. My body is mine. He had no right pressuring* me to send him a picture of my breasts. I need to believe in myself. I wish I'd told my mom right away, when he sent me the text."

Nonnie said, "Thank you, Annie. You've learned a great deal. May I tell your mom what you said? I think you're ready to be trusted." Annie was thrilled and, of course, said yes.

Alex said, "Some kids at school make fun of Ethan now."

Annie was quiet, then said softly, "Maybe he needs to learn about respect and sexuality."

 AcademyPress ~ www.healthyteens.com

Nonnie was thoughtful, then she asked, "Are you ready to finish this Circle?"

The three young people said, yes. Nonnie asked, "Can you guess why the words 'withholding sex' are part of this Circle?"

Alex asked, "What does it mean to withhold sex?'

Nonnie said, "Imagine two people. One wants to connect sexually. The other wants to connect, but also wants something from the person. Sex becomes a tool used to get that something."

The children looked at her, confused.

Nonnie said, "Think of it like this—a person may say 'yes' to sex or say 'no' to sex. Both responses are OK, depending on the person and the situation. Using sex—or withholding sex—to get something from a person isn't OK."

Alex asked, "How can you know what people want?'

Nonnie asked, "What do you think?"

 AcademyPress ~ www.healthyteens.com

Tamika thought about her question. "Maybe you can tell by the way people look?"

Alex agreed. "Maybe by body language*?"

Nonnie showed the children some pictures of couples. "Can you tell if these people are happy?"

Annie said, "I'm not sure. Could it seem as if one of them is trying to talk the other person into something?"

Tamika said, "Their body language looks tense."

Alex added, "Maybe they're just tired."

Annie said, "Or annoyed."

Nonnie said, "I'm so impressed with you three! Body language can be unclear."

Alex sighed. "I think it's easier to just talk together!"

Annie and Tamika thought Alex was correct!

Nonnie smiled, "Good communication is best."

111 AcademyPress ~ www.healthyteens.com

Nonnie looked at the children with affection*. "I'm pleased with the way you talked about this Circle of Sexuality," she said. "Some of the topics in this Circle aren't easy. Do you have any questions or things you want to say?"

Annie said, "I do. If we all respect each other, none of these things would happen."

Nonnie reminded herself to speak with Annie's mom that afternoon. She felt the conversation would go well. Nonnie smiled. "Here are the Sexualization Circle topics," she said.

♦ Advertising (selling a product using sexuality)

♦ Flirting (acting as if a person is attracted to someone, but not in a serious way)

♦ Incest (sex between people who are closely related)

♦ Rape (forcing someone to do sexual things)

♦ Seduction (tempting someone to have sex)

♦ Sexual Harassment (unwelcome sexual advances, often in the workplace)

♦ Withholding Sex (using sexuality in a relationship to get things from a person by denying sexual contact)

    AcademyPress ~ www.healthyteens.com

What Do YOU Think?

The topics in the Sexualization Circle may be difficult to discuss.

How did you feel when you learned about these topics?
Who are your trusted adults?
How do you know they can be trusted?
Please share your thoughts with a trusted adult.

Please draw
or write your
thoughts
here:

AcademyPress ~ www.healthyteens.com

Tamika, Annie, and Alex prepared for their final meeting with Nonnie. Their days were very busy with school and friends. They no longer were in trouble. Their phones were returned. They talked openly with their parents about the Circles of Sexuality. Life was good.

They met Nonnie at the Common Ground Teen Center she runs. It was Middle School Night, and 5th-and 6th-graders were invited. They gathered in the Quiet Room.

Alex said, "I want to be a peer educator so much, Nonnie." "Me, too," said Tamika. Annie said, "And, me."

Nonnie said, "You teach now! Our peer educators just did a panel on racism for the local news-paper. I'm proud of them."

AcademyPress ~ www.healthyteens.com

Chapter Twelve: The Intimacy Circle

Nonnie said, "I believe, when our peer educators teach, their message is heard as a shout; when an older person teaches, the same message is a whisper."

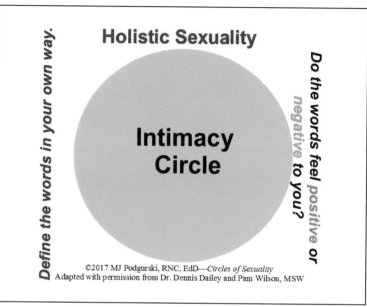

Holistic Sexuality

Define the words in your own way.

Intimacy Circle

Do the words feel positive or negative to you?

©2017 MJ Podgurski, RNC, EdD—*Circles of Sexuality*
Adapted with permission from Dr. Dennis Dailey and Pam Wilson, MSW

She smiled and said, "The final Circle of Sexuality is the Intimacy Circle. Do you have any idea what the word intimacy means?"

Tamika guessed, "Is it about feeling close to someone?"

"Very good, Tamika," Nonnie said. "I saved this Circle for last because it's such a positive one. It begins with caring."

"My word for this Circle is love, Nonnie," said Alex. "How do you know when you're in love?"

Nonnie grinned, "Wow! What a great question. What do you think?"

"You think about the person all the time," said Tamika. "In a good way, not a creepy way."

AcademyPress ~ www.healthyteens.com

"You feel happy when you're together," Annie said.

"I'm happy when I'm with my dog," said Alex. "I love him, but I don't LOVE him!"

Tamika laughed, then said, "How about if you really care for another person?"

Nonnie asked, "What is caring?"

Alex said, "Being there for another person. Being kind."

Annie said, "But, if you're 'in love,' shouldn't you feel kind of super happy? Maybe you hear music?"

Tamika said, "Or, your stomach could feel sick! Maybe you feel shaky?"

Alex snorted. "You watch too many movies! How do you know when you're in love, Nonnie?"

Nonnie said, "I believe love is a feeling. Feelings are very tough to define. It's different for each person. If you feel you are in love, then you are. The love may not be mature love*, though. It may not be a healthy love."

"What's mature love?" asked Tamika.

 AcademyPress ~ www.healthyteens.com

"Mature love isn't about age. A person of any age can have a mature love. It can be other-directed," Nonnie said. "Can you guess what I mean?"

Tamika thought a moment. "Like, if you need something, the person you love will understand and support you?" Annie added, "Maybe the person loves you as you are."

"Yes," Nonnie grinned. "I may need to re-think our age for officially being trained as a peer educator! You're great! Tell me a stress in life."

Annie said, "Having a big test."
Tamika said, "Missing a big goal and losing the game."

Nonnie nodded. "In a mature, healthy relationship, two people support one another. One person would help the other find time to study. One person would listen after a big soccer loss."

Alex said softly, "In a mature love relationship, people don't say 'I love you' unless they mean it."

Nonnie agreed. "Too often 'I love you' is insincere*."

 AcademyPress ~ www.healthyteens.com

Annie asked, "What else makes a love mature and healthy?"

"Guess," said Nonnie.

"Being able to fight nice," Alex said. "My dad talks about disagreeing and still respecting each other."

Nonnie said, "I'm glad your dad teaches you how to be a good partner, Alex. Anything else?"

"My Aunt Janell broke up with a guy once because he wanted to change her." Tamika said.

Alex said, "That's not OK. No one is perfect. Or the same."

{ perfectly imperfect }

Tamika grinned, "That's for sure."

Nonnie said, "Great talk about love! The Intimacy Circle includes a lot of the things we've discussed, like sharing and liking or loving someone. Intimacy includes trust. It also includes self-disclosure. Do you know what it would mean to disclose to a loved one?"

Annie said, "To share something personal." She shrugged. "Like, someday I may tell someone I love about the pics."

118

   AcademyPress ~ www.healthyteens.com

Nonnie said, "I'm proud of the way you've grown, Annie. Can you think of some examples of intimacy in your lives?"

Alex said, "When I spend time with my sister."

Nonnie smiled, "Yes, spending time with Alisia is a loving relationship. It's a family, sibling relationship, but it's not a sexually intimate one. Do you see the difference?"

Alex laughed. "Of course!"

Annie said, "What about when two people are together a long time? My Mom and Dad have been with each other 20 years. They met when my Mom was in med school and waited to have me until she finished. My Dad said it was a 'real trip'." She grinned. "I think supporting someone through lots of years of school and loans is intimate!"

119 AcademyPress ~ www.healthyteens.com

Nonnie said, "I agree."

Alex asked, "How long are you and Pop-pop married?"

Nonnie smiled. "We were married in 1973." Alex whistled, "Man. You are old!" Tamika gave him a mock punch on the arm, and asked, "Are all the topics in the Intimacy Circle positive ones?"

Nonnie said, "Someone might consider vulnerability* negative. What do you think?"

"Does vulnerability mean you could get hurt?" asked Annie softly. "Like after a break up?"

"My Mom was hurt when my Dad left her for my Step-mom," Alex said. He suddenly looked sad, remembering.

Nonnie said, "I remember, Alex. I'm sure it's a difficult memory for you. Yes, being vulnerable may mean a person could be hurt. It is also one of the few ways we allow ourselves to open up and be known by someone. Falling in love and caring about another person makes us vulnerable in a good way."

  AcademyPress ~ www.healthyteens.com

Alex nodded, thinking. Nonnie added, "Another area that might be negative is risk-taking*. It's complicated."

"Why?" Annie was curious.

Nonnie said, "Taking a risk may include opening up and sharing with a person. If the relationship ends, and trust ends, secrets could be shared with others."

Alex said, "Yes! One of our older friends was hurt after a break up. His ex told everyone their secrets."
"Why did they break up?" Annie asked.

"The ex was jealous*," said Tamika. "Our friend was told how to dress and which friends were OK. After texting, he was asked things like 'why aren't you texting me back?' and 'what are you doing?' He was right to break up, but it was still tough."

Nonnie listened. "Relationships can be complicated."

Annie said softly, "Taking risks can get people in trouble." Nonnie agreed. "Risk taking is especially difficult when people are young and their brains aren't finished developing." Tamika sputtered, "Wait a minute. What do you mean? My brain isn't finished growing?" Tamika was shocked. So were Alex and Annie.

 AcademyPress ~ www.healthyteens.com

Nonnie smiled. "Don't panic. Your brains are developing every day. Your prefrontal cortex* is the part of your brain in charge of decision making* and impulse control*. Impulse control helps us deal with urges and temptation*."

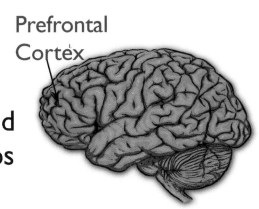
Prefrontal Cortex

"No wonder 6th-graders can make lousy decisions," Annie mumbled.

Tamika suddenly got excited. "I have a great example of intimacy," she said. "My brother LeBron just proposed." She laughed, "My dad had a big talk with him. My word for this Circle came from listening to them. It's responsibility*."

"A good word." Nonnie said, "It means taking of what needs done. Annie, what's your word for this Circle?"

Annie said, "I didn't have one until now. I pick unselfish. It means putting others first."

122 AcademyPress ~ www.healthyteens.com

"Nice one," said Alex. Nonnie smiled again. "I've enjoyed spending time with you. My word today is education!"

"Wait," said Annie. "Are we finished with our meetings? I don't want them to end."

"We can still get together, Annie," said Nonnie. "I think you've worked through your lessons about sending nude pics, though. What do you think?"

Annie said, "I think so. I'm talking with my parents about the Circles and they're trusting me again. I know right from wrong." Nonnie agreed and said, "Here are the Intimacy Circle topics:"

♦ Caring (showing kindness or concern for others)

♦ Loving/Liking (feeling a desire to spend time with someone or feeling deep emotions of love)

♦ Risk Taking (taking chances, especially emotionally)

♦ Self-Disclosure (revealing something difficult)

♦ Sharing (giving something to another)

♦ Trust (believing in someone)

♦ Vulnerability (being exposed to possible hurt)

 AcademyPress ~ www.healthyteens.com

What Do YOU Think?

The topics in the Intimacy Circle
are different from the
other Circles.

How did these topics make you feel?
Do you think a person in love is vulnerable?
Why or why not? Do you think love is tough to define?

Please draw
or write your
thoughts
here:

124

AcademyPress ~ www.healthyteens.com

Chapter Thirteen: Forgiveness and Respect

Annie waited to talk with Nonnie alone when the children gathered to leave. She spoke with Nonnie quietly. Nonnie nodded.

A week later, Nonnie called Tamika and Alex. She asked them to join her at the park near their homes. When they arrived, they were surprised to see Nonnie there with two other children.

Annie and Ethan were with Nonnie! Tamika and Alex joined them. Tamika just stared. Alex asked, "What's up?

It was Ethan who spoke. "Nonnie talked with my dad over a month ago. I've been meeting with her. Annie suggested we all get together."

Annie said, "We're learning to forgive."

Ethan added, "And we're learning to respect each other."

Tamika said, "I think this is the best way to end our meetings."

AcademyPress ~ www.healthyteens.com

Alex grinned. "Ethan," he said, "Tamika, Annie and I are becoming peer educators." He asked Nonnie, "Is it OK if we help teach?"

Nonnie beamed, "Yes, of course, as long as it's OK with Ethan." Ethan agreed.

Annie said, "First, we set our guidelines." She said to Ethan, "Guidelines are the promises we make when we start to teach. The first one is respect." Alex added, "We create them ourselves."

Tamika asked, "What guidelines would make you feel safe, Ethan?"

Nonnie listened as the children created a safe space for learning, right there in the park!

The children took turns sharing the most important things they learned. They tossed a koosh ball from person to person as they spoke. The person holding the ball shared.

Tamika said, "I figured out sexuality is a lot more than just having sex." She tossed the ball to Alex.

  AcademyPress ~ www.healthyteens.com

Alex caught the ball and said, "I learned holistic means the whole of something, and holistic sexuality means we look at the whole of sexual health." He tossed the ball to Annie. Annie caught the ball, and said, "I learned to respect and love my body."

Annie looked at Ethan. He nodded, and reached for the ball as she tossed it to him. He almost had it, but missed. It fell to the ground. Everyone was quiet, and then Ethan said, "I learned to pick myself up when I fall down," as he bent to pick up the ball.

Alex groaned, "I think that was the cheesiest analogy* ever!!" The four children laughed and Ethan threw the ball to Tamika.

AcademyPress ~ www.healthyteens.com

When Tamika caught her breath after laughing and catching the ball, she tried to look serious.

"Nonnie," she said, "did we break a guideline promise? We're supposed to laugh, but not at one another." Ethan snorted, "I laughed, too. It was funny. Right, Nonnie?"

Nonnie agreed. Then the children talked together while Nonnie watched them. Sometimes they asked her a question, but most of the time they worked things out together.

Nonnie was very happy.

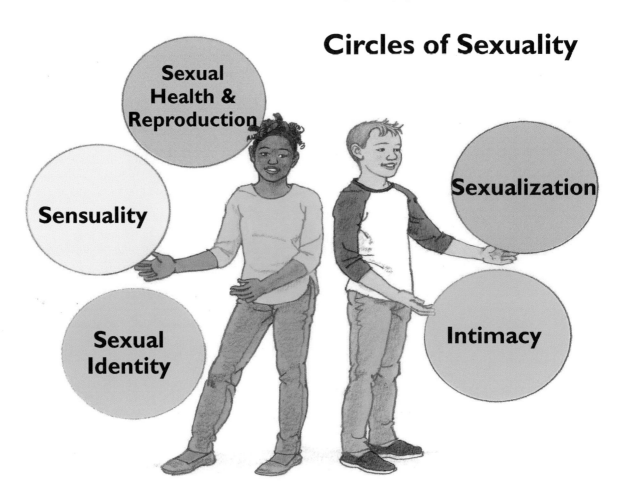

Circles of Sexuality

Sexual Health & Reproduction

Sensuality

Sexual Identity

Sexualization

Intimacy

AcademyPress ~ www.healthyteens.com

What Do YOU Think?

Did you enjoy learning about sexuality and more?

What was your favorite Circle of Sexuality?
Which Circle was the most difficult to discuss?
If you were creating Circles of Sexuality,
would you add one?

Please draw
or write your
thoughts
here:

129

AcademyPress ~ www.healthyteens.com

Glossary

Abuelita: Grandmother. Tamika's grandfather immigrated from the Dominican Republic and she calls her grandmother abuelita because she was married to him.

Abuelito: Grandfather. See above.

Accepted: Believed as OK.

Advertisement: Something used to sell a product.

Advertising: Producing messages to sell something.

Affection: A feeling of fondness or liking someone.

AIDS: Acquired immunedeficiency syndrome. A disease that hurts the immune system (the part of the body that fights infection).

Allies: Individuals who support other groups of people unlike themselves. Allies need to listen to those for whom they give support. Allies are not in charge.

Analogy: Comparing two things that are alike in some way.

Annoying: Troubling or disturbing to someone.

Anxious: Feeling fear or nervousness, especially about something that will happen.

Approach: One way to do something (in this context).

Asexual: A person who may not be interested in intercourse or sexual contact.

Assisted-Living Facility: Housing where people live and receive the help they need while still enjoying some independence.

Attraction: Feeling drawn to someone because of physical looks or personality.

Behavior: The way a person acts, especially around other people.

Binary: Related to two things; within sexual orientation, attracted to more than one gender.

Bisexual: See binary.

Body Language: Communicating without words.

Body Image: How people see themselves.

130

Glossary

Calm: When a person is free from excitement or anger.

Certified: Proven to be able to do something well.

Challenging: Testing one's ability to face something or do something.

Chlamydia: A bacterial STI that is often silent.

Circles of Sexuality: A holistic way to look at sexuality as a whole, considering all parts of sexual health and wellness.

Cisgender: A gender identity where self-identity is the same as body parts.

Community: A social group; in this book, the children and Nonnie create a community.

Complicated: Difficult to understand or explain.

Condom: A thin cover, usually made of latex, that is placed over the penis to lower risk from unplanned pregnancy and STI spread.

Confidentiality: Keeping a trust. What happens in a group, stays with the group.

Confused: Feeling unclear or unsure about something.

Connection: Linking or bonding together.

Consent: To permit or allow; to say yes.

Consequences: The result of something.

Contract: An agreement between two people agreeing to something.

Controversial: Subject to debate or public disagreement.

Conversation: Talking; communication between people.

Culture: Beliefs, customs, and traditions of a particular place, group of people, or society.

Curious: Eager to learn or know something.

Death: The end of life.

AcademyPress ~ www.healthyteens.com

Glossary

Decision Making: Making choices.

Detention: A consequence for behavior, often imposed on students in schools.

Embarrassing: Feeling shame or discomfort.

Emotions: Feelings.

Empathy: Connecting with others; seeking understanding of another's experience.

Encountered: Come upon or meeting someone.

Encouragement: To inspire with spirit or confidence.

Erection: When a body part, like a penis, fills with blood and becomes hard.

Ethics: Moral principles of rules of conduct.

Fair: Free from bias, judgment or dishonesty.

Fallopian tubes: Two tubes along which the eggs (ova) travel from the ovary to the uterus.

Fantasy: In someone's imagination; mental images.

Fertility: The ability to conceive (make) children.

Fertilization: When an egg and a sperm unite for conception.

Flirting: To act attracted to someone without serious intentions.

Forgiveness: Giving pardon to someone.

Freak: A person or thing different from nature; a monster. In youth culture, someone different. Freak could be used as a put down, but may also be embraced.

Gay: Someone who is attracted physically or emotionally or both, to another as self.   gender

Gender: Roles, behavior and activities a society makes OK for men and women.

Gender Fluid: People who do not conform (fit into) the stereotypes associated with their sex assigned at birth.

AcademyPress ~ www.healthyteens.com

Glossary

Genitals: Sexual body parts.

Glared: Stared at someone with a fierce look.

Gonorrhea: A sexually transmitted infection caused by the bacteria gonococcus.

Gracias: "Thank you" in Spanish.

Gratitude: Feeling thankful.

Grief: Mourning after a loss.

Grounded: A term for a consequence sometimes given to young people, where they are not permitted varying social experiences.

Guilt: Feeling badly after doing something wrong.

Herpes: A viral sexually transmitted infection caused by the herpes simplex viruses.

Holistic: The idea that the whole is more than the sum of its parts.

Holistic Sexuality: Looking at the whole of sexuality, as demonstrated in the Circles of Sexuality.

Honesty: Telling the truth.

Hormones: Chemical messengers inside the body produced by the endocrine system.

HIV: Human immunodeficiency virus; the virus that cause AIDS.

HPV: Human papillomavirus; a sexually transmitted infection caused by a virus.

Human: Person.

Identical: Exactly the same.

Identity: Who or what a person or thing is.

Infertility: Unable to conceive (make) children.

Illegal: Against the law.

Impatient: Restless or tired of waiting.

AcademyPress ~ www.healthyteens.com

Glossary

Influence: The power to make people rethink their opinions or behavior.

Impulse Control: The ability to put off quick choices based on urges or temptations.

Indefinitely: Without end.

Insincere: Not honest in expressing feelings.

Integrity: Positive moral character; honesty.

Interconnected: Linked or bonded together, yet separate.

Intercourse: One way of having sex.

Intersex: An individual born with both male and female genitals.

Jackpot: In gambling, a huge win.

Jealous: In a relationship, feeling or showing unfaithfulness towards a partner.

Junk: Garbage. In youth culture, may be a slang for genitals.

Lesbian: Women attracted physically and emotionally to women.

Legal: Within the law.

Life-span: Across a person's life, from birth to death.

Lust: Strong attraction or sexual desire.

Masturbation: Touching one's own genitals for pleasure.

Mature Love: Love that is other-directed (unselfish), supportive of the partner, nurturing and accepting of difference in the partner. Not based on a person's age.

Medically Accurate: Proven by science and accepted by medical practitioners.

Medicine: The art and science of preserving life.

Michelangelo's David: A famous sculpture created by Michelangelo, Italian Renaissance sculptor, painter, architect, and poet.

Miserable: Very unhappy, uneasy or uncomfortable.

134

Glossary

Mistake: An error.

Moody: When people's moods or feelings swing from happy to sad to angry to excited.

Moral Compass: Values that guide a person to make ethical decisions.

Moral Principles: Principles of right and wrong accepted by an individual or society.

Myths: Story spread without factual base.

Non-Binary: Refers to gender identity that is not male or female.

Non-Conforming: In the context of gender, not adhering to typical genders.

Normal: Typical.

Nude Pic: Common slang in youth culture used to describe a picture of a naked person sent via a cellphone or online device.

Opinions: Views on something, not based on facts.

Oral Sex: Sexual contact involving mouth to genitals.

Orgasm: A climax of sexual excitement, accompanied by sexual pleasure. Sexual pleasure may happen with or without an orgasm.

Ovum: An egg; one half of the cells needed to create life. The other is a sperm.

Own the Message: Nonnie wants her students to make the messages in her lessons part of their lives by owning her messages.

Pansexual: A person who identifies as pansexual doesn't limit partners based on gender or gender identity or biological sex.

Parenting Lottery: A term Nonnie created to explain how lucky she was to be born into a nurturing family.

Peer Education: Teens trained to teach other teens or peers.

Penis: A sensitive part of genitals in bodies with boy parts; for pleasure, reproduction, and elimination.

AcademyPress ~ www.healthyteens.com

Glossary

Permission: Seeking or giving consent.

Photoshopped: Using computer software to change photos.

Pleasure: A feeling of happiness and enjoyment.

Porn or Pornography: Visual materials showing graphic sexual acts.

Prefrontal Cortex: The part of the brain that covers impulse control.

Pressuring: Using coercion to make someone do something.

Privacy: Time spent alone.

Process: After teaching, discussion about the content.

Product: Something made for sale.

Puberty: Emotional and physical growth from child to adult.

Racism: When people are judged by the color of their skin or their race.

Regret: Feeling badly about something.

Research: Scientific studies demonstrating facts.

Responsibility: Something that needs to be done.

Risk Taking: Doing something that involves danger or risk.

Role Model: A person who sets an example to be duplicated.

Sensuality: The enjoyment of physical pleasure.

Society: People living together in a community.

Sperm: A male reproductive cell. When united by fertilization with a female ovum, can create an embryo (the start of a baby).

STIs: Sexually transmitted infections. Infections primarily spread through sexual contact.

Suspended: In this context, when a student is made to take days off from school.

136

Glossary

Symptoms: Signs of illness.

Syphilis: A bacterial STI caused by the spirochete treponema pallidum bacteria.

Temptations: Things people want or activities people want to do, but should not.

Testicles: The part of the body where sperm are made.

Transgender: A person whose gender identity is different from their biological sex.

Trusted Adult: An adult with whom a child is safe; someone who listens and protects a child.

Unique: One of a kind.

Uterus: The part of a body where a pregnancy occurs and a fetus grows. A womb.

Vagina: Passage between the vulva and the uterus.

Vulnerability: Being exposed for hurt, either physical or emotional.

Vulva: External female genitals.

Wisdom: Having experience, knowledge and good judgment.

Worthy: Deserving respect.

 AcademyPress ~ www.healthyteens.com

Endorsements

Dr. Mary Jo Podgurski has an incredible gift for talking with children in a way that they can understand and feel cared about at the same time. Please give this book to every family you know that has a child in this age range. The topics are tender and real. Reading it together will foster communication that can continue on into the teen years. I highly recommend it.

Betsy Crane, Ph.D., Professor,
Center for Human Sexuality Studies,
Widener University

It is extremely rewarding to have ones work put to such creative and thoughtful use. Nothing is more difficult than finding a way to connect to children and adolescents about sexuality as a part off the life they live. Mary Jo has produced a book that I think can do just that tough job. Why? Because she writes about the contemporary world of young people. Above all she is not condescending (something young people can spot a mile off). She is honest and straight forward (read she does not lie to kids). This is a book that should be in every family library and shared in the family context. Maybe more importantly, this is a book that every sexuality educator should read if they aspire to be NONNIE in the lives of those they teach and learn from. There is much to be learned by all.

Dennis Dailey, DSW
Author of the Circles of Sexuality

Dr. Podgurski's most recent book, Nonnie Talks About Sex...And More!" is a brilliant and compelling addition to the sex education field. She covers meaningful topics like sexuality, consent, and cybersafety in a compassionate and accessible manner. This book will be a meaningful resource for teachers, parents, and guardians to speak honestly with children about their sexual development.

Shadeen Francis, MFT
Therapist, Speaker, Educator

If you are a caring adult who feels even a little bit of anxiety about having the Big Talk - about SEX! - with young people in your life, you want Nonnie by your side. Mary Jo Podgurski, EdD (aka "Nonnie") has once again shown us how to bravely combine wisdom, wit, kindness and respect to convey complex ideas to young people. Thank you, Dr. P!

Joan Garrity
Consultant and Trainer

138

Endorsements

Nonnie Talks About Sex...& More is a warm and sensitively written book. It's a wonderful guide to help pre-teens think through the various aspects of sexuality in today's world. Its interactive lessons are great tools to foster communication between young people and their parents or other trusted adults, and it's an excellent way to support young people's healthy sexual development. If you have fifth-to-eighth graders in your life, you need this book.

Michael McGee, PhD
Assistant Professor, Health Education Borough of
Manhattan Community College

"Nonnie" has done it again. Mary Jo Podgurski (the brains and gentle heart and loving soul behind Nonnie) has written another marvelous book to help young people decipher the confusing world of sexuality. Part of the excellence and uniqueness of this book is her focus on the importance of giving children a vocabulary to help them talk about sexual issues. And that – COMMUNICATION – is what we sexuality educators and therapists consistently stress as the *sine qua non* for a healthy approach to this wonderful – and critical – and often confusing topic – sexuality. Get it – for your children and grandchildren.

Robert Selverstone, Ph.D.
Licensed Psychologist

Nonnie knows that sexuality is a complex and dynamic concept, and breaks it down into clear, easy to understand chunks by using Dennis Dailey's Circles of Sexuality. The Circles allow Nonnie (and her readers) to start the conversation with whatever circle seems most important at the moment, and to build from there until the whole of sexuality unfolds. I know this is a book that parents and trusted adults will come back to again and again to mine its wealth of information and its excellent modeling of how to talk to children about this essential aspect of being human.

Al Vernacchio, Sexuality Educator, Author of *For Goodness Sex: Changing the Way We Talk to Teens about Sexuality, Values and Health*

Endorsements

Nonnie Talks About Sex and More begins with two sixth graders returning to their respective homes at the end of a school day, furious. Each storms past family members on their way to their room and slams the door shut behind them. Wow, I thought, a story about "sex and more" that begins with anger and non-communication! I smiled and relaxed knowing this is a book about sex that I can trust.

Every time Mary Jo Podgurski takes on a topic in her Nonnie series, I know it will bring me to a new level of awareness. This is true even when I've explored the subject myself, in my personal life and professional writing. Dr. Podgurski is unafraid of her material, no matter how many layers must be sorted through so that kids can better relate to the challenges they face. This book is no exception and we enter into an honest dialogue about "sex and more" with a texting scandal that has rocked the sixth grade.

Then Dr. Podgurski does her excellent work. She draws all members of the family into the conversation in whatever way is most appropriate for them. Even the older brother LeBron, away at college, gets a call that lets him know he's on duty as an elder who can help bear witness to and support a younger sibling who needs it. In fact, it's a while into the story before Nonnie is even called. Kids have already been grounded, parents have checked in with each other, and the principal has called everyone to the office to confront the issue together.

No one is more prepared to address the "more" that is included in the title than Nonnie. This book about sex is also about privacy, feeling loved, expressing consent, wanting connection, wanting information, and wanting to be wanted. It's about shame, disclosure, exposure, and fear. It's about safety, clarity, integrity, identity. So yeah, it's about sex and everything that comes with it.

As usual, Dr. Podgurski makes sure the kids get to speak for themselves: "What you hear on the bus isn't always the truth," reminds Tamika. "My mom thinks phones are evil," laments Alex. Even the kids most central to the troubling incident are invited into the story, in person and in communication with their peers, to receive the warmth and belonging that Nonnie shows every person within her reach, all of the time, no matter what. In doing so, Nonnie deftly moves each child off-line as a target for blame, choosing to foster their awareness, empathy, and connection instead.

"How do you know what to teach?" one of the children asks Nonnie. "I listen to young people to find out what they need," she replies. In Nonnie Talks About Sex and More, Dr. Podgurski applies what she knows young people need most of all in order to be safe and fulfilled: their own authority.

This is the book where Nonnie mentors Alex and Tamika to become peer educators. Having seen these characters grow up in the Nonnie series – curious about death, curious about gender, curious about race – I got chills as Nonnie reflected back to them, slowly and expertly throughout the story, the full extent of their self-knowledge and capacity to show kindness and take responsibility. Not only is she not mad at them, as they feared she might be, she is ready to trust them more than ever.

Anastasia Higginbotham, author of *Tell Me About Sex, Grandma*

140

          AcademyPress ~ www.healthyteens.com

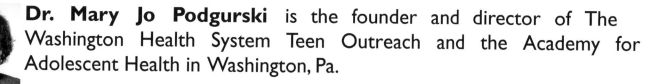

Dr. Mary Jo Podgurski is the founder and director of The Washington Health System Teen Outreach and the Academy for Adolescent Health in Washington, Pa.

She is a nurse, a counselor, a parent, a trainer, an author, a speaker, and an educator who is dedicated to serving young people.

The Outreach has reached over 230,000 young people since 1988. Check out www.healthyteens.com for information on the Academy and its programs.

Dr. Podgurski is certified as a childbirth educator through Lamaze International, as a sexuality educator and a sexuality counselor through AASECT (American Association for Sexuality Educators, Counselors and Therapists), as an Olweus Bullying Prevention Program trainer and through Parents As Teachers.

She is an authorized facilitator for the Darkness to Light abuse prevention program. Mary Jo is the author of the *Ask Mary Jo* weekly column in the Observer-Reporter newspaper and answers 6—10 questions from young people daily. She wrote *Nonnie Talks about Gender* as a labor of love and the *Nonnie Series* was birthed!

Most important, Mary Jo and her partner Rich are the parents of three wonderful adult children and are blessed to be grandparents. She is a Nonnie in Real Life!

Dr. Podgurski believes ally is a verb.
She believes in social and racial justice.
She believes in young people.
She believes each person is a person of worth. Please pass it on.

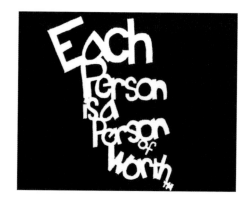

 AcademyPress ~ www.healthyteens.com

ABOUT THE NONNIE SERIES

The NonnieSeries

Writing *Nonnie Talks about Gender* in the summer of 2014 was a true labor of love. The idea of a "Nonnie Series" never entered my mind.

The reactions I've had to *Nonnie Talks about Gender* surprised and humbled me. I began to realize gender wasn't the only challenging topic in our world. Social media and 24 hour news have created information overload, where even elementary school children are inundated with potentially confusing and troubling subjects. How should adults open the door to these teachable moments?

As a young nurse I became a birth advocate; as a certified Lamaze childbirth educator I have continued my commitment to birthing women and families since the 1970s. In 1973, I began working with pediatric oncology at Memorial Sloan Kettering Cancer Center in New York City. My passion for birthing normally dovetailed with my growing commitment for death with dignity. I became a hospice nurse in the 1980s. Long before the "circle of life" became part of a popular film for children, I learned how vital birth and death are to the human behavior, and how often both topics are avoided when talking with children.

With birth and death advocacy as my foundation, I decided to tackle these subjects in books for children as part of a series based on the "Nonnie" concept. I started storyboards on both topics. Then, life intervened.

As an ally and advocate for racial and social justice, I cannot ignore how much our culture needs to address racial equity. Then, as I was presenting my child abuse prevention program, *Inside Out, Your Body is Amazing Inside and Out and Belongs Only to YOU*, an eight-year-old child told me what #BlackLivesMatter meant to her. We talked, I listened. This little one's very real fear that her own life was less worthy than another's based on the color of her skin was my inspiration for *Nonnie Talks about Race*.

Nonnie Talks about Puberty was born because another child needed it. I began teaching growing up classes called What's Up as You Grow Up in 1984. Gender non-conforming children are often confused during puberty; I couldn't find an inclusive resource on growing up, so I wrote one. Empathy is a learned skill. I hope all children will benefit from the information in *Nonnie Talks about Puberty*. As a birth advocate since the 1970s, *Nonnie Talks about Pregnancy and Birth* was my next obvious topic. *Nonnie Talks about Death* was a natural result of serving as an RN in pediatric oncology and as a hospice nurse. *Nonnie Talks about Sex…& More* comes from decades of work as an AASECT certified sexuality educator and sexuality counselor. I plan to address mental health and disability next. I have a list of other topics I hope to explore. If you have any ideas for the *Nonnie Series*, or would like to be informed about coming titles, please connect with me at podmj@healthyteens.com.

AcademyPress ~ www.healthyteens.com

Did you enjoy *Nonnie Talks about Sex…& More?*
Need the conversations in *Nonnie Talks about Death?*
Interested in *Nonnie Talks about Puberty?*
Curious about *Nonnie Talks about Race?*
Intrigued by *Nonnie Talks about Pregnancy and Birth?*
Wondering about *Nonnie Talks about Gender?*
Entranced by the concept of the *Nonnie Series?*

Dr. Podgurski has dedicated her life to empowering young people.
She strives to model her motto of "Each Person is a Person of Worth"
through education, writing, and trainings.
She is available for workshops and consultation.
She is also the author of 32 books.
You can find her books, including the Nonnie Series, at Amazon or
on her websites, www.healthyteens.com or
www.drmaryjopodgurski.com
You can reach her at:
Email: podmj@healthyteens.con
http://www.healthyteens.com/
Toll free #: 1 (888) 301-2311
Twitter DrMaryJoPod

143

AcademyPress ~ www.healthyteens.com

Printed in Great Britain
by Amazon